Growing Up
in Heaven

James Van Praagh

Growing Up in Heaven

The Eternal Connection
Between Parent
and Child

HarperOne
An Imprint of HarperCollins*Publishers*

HarperOne

The individual experiences recounted in this book are true. However, many of the names and certain descriptive details have been changed to protect the identities of those involved.

GROWING UP IN HEAVEN: *The Eternal Connection Between Parent and Child*. Copyright © 2011 by James Van Praagh. All rights reserved. Printed in the United States of America. No part of this book may be used or reproduced in any manner whatsoever without written permission except in the case of brief quotations embodied in critical articles and reviews. For information address HarperCollins Publishers, 10 East 53rd Street, New York, NY 10022.

HarperCollins®, ■®, and HarperOne™ are trademarks of HarperCollins Publishers

ISBN 978-0-06-202463-3

To my sister Maura Fortune

Thank you for the love you continue to

demonstrate every day.

You made my childhood better;

you make my life better.

Contents

Introduction

I COMMUNICATE WITH THE DEAD. It is what I do and I am blessed to have this ability. Given the nature of the communication, I am in contact with those who have passed over and gone to heaven on a regular basis. That is, I talk to the dead quite frequently. For this reason, some may think my job is depressing or bleak, but that is far from true. As strange as it may sound, death is a part of life. That is, death is but a stage in the soul's spiritual journey.

My ability, and the job I have chosen on this earthly plane, comes with a great responsibility. It is very important that I help share my knowledge and experience so that those who have lost loved ones can find solace and peace during their souls' journeys. All of us are on a path together. This book is written to help ease the suffering and to shine a light on a world that too few of us know or understand.

Most of us greet the warmth and excitement of the rising sun as the assurance of a new day. But others wake in the morning after a restless sleep, to a day of darkness—a void that we feel can never and will never again be filled. The promise of expectation has been replaced with the painful realization of the loss of future memories. This is the pain of losing a child. Loss of any kind is traumatic, but the loss of a child is truly devastating. It may be the ultimate loss we humans can ever experience on this earth. The symbiotic relationship between a child and its parent is like no other. Perhaps no explanation and understanding can ever be obtained on this physical level. We can try to learn to live with the pain, but such an event alters our lives forever.

For some, it feels as if they will never be able to go on, and that their lives are truly over. Others may attempt to live their lives, but merely trudge along clinging to the hope of a time when they will be reunited with their children. Perhaps that is the only thing they can hold on to in order to get through the bleak days. These folks may spend hours imagining what their children would look like, the kind of personality they would have, and the types of interests and activities they would enjoy.

If you have endured the loss of a baby, child, family member, or friend, this book is my gift to you. The readings and letters contained within may help you to understand that you are never alone in your grief, that your child or loved one is always around to ease your pain, and that it is possible to survive your loss and move forward in a more aware state of mind than ever before—even if you think all of this is impossible at the present moment.

If you have ever wondered what heaven looks and feels like, this book is for you. Many of us may have preconceived ideas or notions about "heaven" as a place with harp-playing angels floating on clouds, or beings walking around in robes singing in choirs. Although I am sure there are places where these things exist, the heaven I speak of is a very different place, and I will show it to you. Prepare yourself to enter a wondrous new dimension. I will take you into a world that is even more magnificent than you could ever possibly conceive—a dimension encompassing vistas of enhanced creativity, and kingdoms of beauty and art unrealized in our limited physical world. It is a world that your soul may somehow remember and, inevitably, a world you will see again.

As you read this book, be aware of the wisdom of the spirits, and go along with the journey. To get the most out of the words accumulated on these pages, view them with the realization that we are first and foremost *spirits* or *souls* encapsulated in physical bodies. Our souls are the entire essence of who we are. The spirit is the ethereal or subtle body created by the soul to experience the sensations and dimensions of various realities.

As a soul you are capable of having a human experience in a physical dimension, but you must realize that this physical world is measured by the limitations of time. The spiritual dimensions, however, are not restricted by clocks, calendars, or anniversaries. To experience them, you will have to forgo "earthly" ideas of time and open yourself to the ways of life in the world of Spirit.

In these pages, I hope to provide answers to the questions you hold deep in your hearts about where the spirits of children go when they leave the earth and how they grow up there. I hope to give you a soul's view of the purpose for life on earth. In the process, we will go deep into the idea of reincarnation, meet the helpful guides of the other world, and ultimately answer the questions about heaven that so many of us have.

Come along with me now. Open the curtain of your mind and step into a world beyond this world. The promise of a new day can be the birth of a new beginning. Anything and everything you can imagine is possible. Each day can be joyful, dramatic, and exhilarating—filled with myriad opportunities. Brand-new experiences and new people, the exploration of far-off and not-so-far-off destinations, and new perspectives await you. All that holds you back are the limitations of your own mind. Together we will explore growing up in heaven.

PART ONE

Crossing Over

When a Child Transitions

When a parent dies, you lose your past;
when a child dies, you lose your future.

—ANONYMOUS

DEATH LEAVES A TRAIL of various states of emotional upheaval and spiritual awakening. The most important thing to realize is that we are never truly alone, even when we think we are. Our loved ones are around to help us through our most painful moments and to guide us out of the darkness and into the light of our own strength.

I was recently at a memorial service for a friend's mother, sitting by myself in the hallway of the funeral home before the ceremony began. I could hear the muffled music and tearful eulogies coming from a nearby room. Suddenly, I saw the spirit of a little girl about seven years old, wearing a light-blue dress, white socks, and black patent-leather shoes. She was skipping up and down the hall. When she went by, she looked at me and

I acknowledged her. She turned around, came back, and stared into my eyes.

Hi Mister. I answered her in my mind. Hi.*Why is my family crying?* Didn't you die? I asked her. *I don't know. I fell asleep and woke up here. The lady with the pink dress and pretty smile is ready to bring me home. There is a pony waiting for me there. I can't wait.* Then why are you here? *I am trying to tell my mommy and daddy I'm still alive, but they don't see me.* What's your name? *Kylie. Isn't it a pretty name?* Suddenly the little girl turned around. *Oops, got to go now! The shiny lady is waiting for me.*

And with that, the girl ran past me toward a glowing spirit on the other side. The spirit greeted the little girl and took her by the hand. Together, they walked into the light of their heavenly home.

Later that day, as I headed toward the parking lot, I noticed a picture on a podium outside a small chapel. I went over to check it out. There was Kylie, sitting on a stack of hay in front of a horse and pony. I smiled, looked upward, and thought to myself: I hope you're enjoying your new pony, Kylie.

I would soon find out what Kylie was doing on the other side.

Through the years, I have counseled thousands of parents who have lost their children. The loss of a child is perhaps the most difficult of all things to comprehend. Parents are in denial and disbelief: "It is not natural that my child died before me. It doesn't make sense!" It is only natural that parents expect their children to grow up, enjoy the jewels life has to offer, and have children of their own one day. This is what we all know as the normal cycle of life. But when a child dies, parents are unhappily forced to rethink everything they once believed about what is "normal," because their lives have been irreparably interrupted by tremendous loss—including the loss of innocence, dreams, and hopes.

Yet loss is a part of life's cycle, and no one can escape it. Loss is part of our life experience and, inevitably, we all must face some kind of loss while we are walking on this earth. It is part of what makes us human. Loss can cause many intense emotions—from sadness, to rage, and even hate—but all these emotions are a natural part of our growing and evolving as a result of the loss. The loss of a child goes deeper because it touches everything in our lives, from our views of the world to the way we feel about those closest to us. Parents often feel as if their child was grabbed from their arms, as though a thief had come in the night and taken away everything they ever had. Many parents' grief can be too intense to bear; and they feel thrown into a place of great emptiness, not sure how they will survive. It is such an extreme paradox. Not only do they have to face the loss of a child, but they must also continue to live their own lives as fully as possible. Thus, bereaved parents deal with the contradictory burden of wanting to be free of their overwhelming pain, while being reminded of the pain every day. How are they supposed to deal with feelings of guilt, anger, and powerlessness, yet move on at the same time? Is it ever possible to recover?

I do believe that everything, no matter how horrendous, happens for a reason and according to a soul's plan. A soul's plan is a unique blueprint for its spiritual evolution. Certain paths in life are chosen by a soul to learn charitable qualities such as compassion, kindness, peacefulness, patience, healing, and harmony. These paths may require endurance and persistence through difficult situations—especially the death of a child. Each challenge is planned so that a person will grow beyond limited human thinking and negative emotional expression. Because every soul has free will, it can choose when and how it will spiritually evolve beyond human imperfection, and it does so through lifetimes of experiences on earth and elsewhere. The ultimate design of a soul's plan is the realization that we are all love created by Love. This is soul enlightenment.

Because our bodies and emotions limit our ability to understand anything beyond our sensory world, we may not be able to understand the meaning behind a death or a loss. However, we must never lose hope that in some way, later on, we may comprehend why such an event had to occur and what its benefits may be.

A Choice to Make

Everyone behaves differently when they lose a child. The reasons for this vary. What were the circumstances of the child's death? Is the family close-knit and supportive, or at odds with one another? Are the parents spiritually evolved or spiritually deficient? We all grieve differently, and no one should ever expect to handle his or her emotional turmoil in the same way someone else does. By observing parents these many years, I have come to know two kinds of parents: those who use their child's death as an opportunity for growth, and those who remain completely and utterly destroyed.

I remember the first time I met Marie Levine. It was in her tiny New York apartment filled with books and photographs. After a detailed reading that yielded facts only she could know, I thought she would be thrilled by what she had learned from her son, Peter, who recently passed into Spirit. Instead, all she could say was: "I can't go on. How am I supposed to live my life? It has no meaning anymore." Even though Marie was in a dark place at that specific moment, I felt that she had more to give if only she would open her heart and mind to the love of her dead son. I stayed in touch with her and, after many years of prodding, a different Marie emerged. She was able to turn her anger and frustration into something positive. The loss of her only son forced her to dig deep inside herself to find healing. She turned her grief into writing and became a wonderful healer for other souls experiencing similar situations. Marie eventually wrote about her devastating loss and her hope to survive in a book entitled *First You Die.*

Marie's words now help many parents face their loneliness and despair with courage. The book became a bestseller and is used in many grief support groups throughout the country. Like Marie, other parents have forged ahead as well. Some have studied metaphysics and spirituality, resulting in more best-selling books. Healing centers, meditation circles, grief support groups, medical information groups, and other positive outcomes have also materialized.

I have also witnessed the opposite. I have known parents so tormented by the loss of their child that they don't feel worthy of living and simply cannot move on. Hilary came to me after her son jumped off the roof of an apartment building in New York. His suicide left her feeling completely abandoned. Hilary could not cope and sat for days and weeks just thinking of her son and what she could have done differently. She blamed herself. She blamed God. She blamed the world. Hilary's tragedy was so overwhelming that her only way out of her pain was to join her son. I learned that she overdosed on sedatives and left behind a suicide note that said: "Life has lost its magic."

Hilary's story is tragic. But no matter the situation—no matter how dark it may feel or be in this very moment—life doesn't have to be this way.

I know many parents who have gone through divorce, drug addiction, gambling addiction, mental health problems, and even hoarding because of their overpowering sense of worthlessness and sorrow. They just seem to spiral downward, unable to recover from their grief. The following messages from the spirit world demonstrate both the depth of the despair and the many ways we can cope with it and get better. The pain and grief are real, and so is the path to healing. I believe sharing these stories is the best way to discover hope and to learn to live and love once again.

The Alcoholic Father

A couple of years ago at one of my demonstrations on the West Coast, I was drawn to a man sitting on the left side of the auditorium. I could tell that there was something unbalanced about him; as I got nearer, I realized that he was drunk. Trying to make light of the situation in front of the large crowd, I said, "Have you been drinking?" He was a little startled by my frankness. I continued, "And why didn't you offer me something?"

The audience laughed, and the tension was relieved. At that moment, I noticed a figure standing behind the man, and I continued with my reading.

"A young man is standing next to you. Do you understand this, please?"

Again, the man was taken aback.

"He is telling me that his head doesn't hurt anymore. He wants you to know that he isn't in pain."

The man had yet to speak, but I could see a tear roll down his face.

"This is your son, isn't it? Do you understand? It's Michael."

"Michael . . . we called him Mike," he finally said.

"Mike is showing me a small plane." Suddenly, Mike sent me a picture of what had happened. I saw him flying through the clouds going faster and faster.

The man, whom I came to know as Jack, blurted out, "He died skydiving."

A woman next to the man grabbed his hand.

Jack continued. "Mike loved the feeling of being free. He was with his friends. They were all part of a skydiving team. His parachute didn't work, and he . . ." He could not say the words.

I moved closer to Mike's father. "He is saying that he is all right now."

"Thank you."

"Your son says he was with you in the garage the other day. He wants you to know that he remembers the good times you had working on the car."

Jack nodded in understanding.

"Your son is saying that he has been working through you to help others who have a drinking problem."

Upon hearing this, the father became somewhat flustered.

"He wants you to know that he is helping you, too. *You have to stop drinking, Dad,* he is saying. *It's hurting everyone around you.*"

There was a pause. Then I turned to Jack and added, "Your son thanks you for the tattoo. He thinks it's awesome. Do you understand?"

The man pulled up his T-shirt and across his entire chest were the words: My Beloved Son Michael.

Several months later, Mike's father showed up at another one of my demonstrations. "Do you remember me?" he asked. "Sure I do. Your son was a skydiver."

"I want you to meet some other members of my family." Jack then introduced several people standing next to him. They took turns shaking my hand and making me feel appreciated.

"I just want to thank you. You have given me the courage to go on. Because of my son, I started AA and have been sober for sixty-three days. I can feel Mike around me and I know he is helping me. I plan to keep up his work. Together we are going to assist anyone with a drinking problem. I made a promise to Mike that my goal for the rest of my life would be to fulfill his work on earth."

Don't Be Afraid

If you ask a thousand people to share their thoughts about life and death, you will get a thousand different answers. Every person is unique, and everyone's life experiences differ. Besides, as I will discuss, each of us is at a distinct stage of soul development, so we are not all on the same page in understanding the purpose of our soul's plan and the intentions and preparations we make before coming to earth to fulfill it.

Michael helped his father think differently and therefore enabled him to help others heal and find a new way of living. Those of us left on earth must always adjust to the death of loved ones, and this is not always easy.

No matter the cause, death is basically a transition from one life to the next. It can come quickly or be drawn out, but in either case, there is a change. Most of us feel that we can control the amount of change around us. Unfortunately, there is so much in life that is beyond our control. Nothing stays the same and the world we live in is constantly in flux.

For many parents, the loss of a child also means another change. So many parents lose their own sense of identity— "Who am I without my child?" Parents can feel incapable of living life without their children because it suddenly seems they have lost themselves as well.

For years, I have worked with parents of deceased children and I know that if they do not go through the necessary grieving process—giving themselves adequate time to mourn their loss and find themselves again—the consequences are usually negative. When parents try to hold back their emotions and don't express how they feel about the death of a child, a wave of emotions overwhelms them, like a snowball rolling downhill, picking up mass and speed as it goes.

For the first several days, weeks, and months of grief, parents are often in a kind of robotic phase—receiving condolences, making arrangements, calling relatives, busying themselves with any little thing they can to keep themselves from the reality of the situation. They are numb. Their self-esteem is destroyed. The significant role with which they so closely identified is gone.

You may think that because parents experience so much in their children's lives, a child's death would bring the family closer together. All too often, it does just the opposite. The death of a child forever changes the dynamic between a husband and wife, and between parents and their living children. A major social adjustment is required in everyone's relationship. Of course, there is some consolation in the fact that they have each other to share the grief, but parents also seem to have unrealized expectations of each other. Usually, each wants the other to lessen the grief and stop the hurt, but it is impossible to heal another person if you cannot stop the hurt within yourself.

One of the most common effects of this hurt is blame. One parent blames the other for "not watching out" or "not doing what you said you would do." At first, one parent may assume blame for the death of his child: "If only I had been a better father, this wouldn't have happened." Or, "If only I hadn't given him the car keys, he never would have had that accident!" Then the blame is turned on the other parent: "If you had been home more watching over him, this never would have happened!" Or, "What kind of a mother are you to allow your daughter to hang out with people like that?" Unfortunately, I have been around parents and heard them say these exact words to one another. After a while, resentment sets in.

If parents do not work through their grief, their feelings of anger, blame, and resentment turn into self-loathing, sleeplessness, and depression, and can lead to drug and alcohol addiction. It is very important that parents express their feelings as often as they can. Death is not a favorite or easy subject to discuss. But in order for us to be healthy, it must be discussed, and feelings must be shared—especially between partners.

Unable to Cope

Stacey could not share her feelings, and was in deep denial when she came to one of my events in Vancouver. The first thing that struck me when I saw her sitting in the back of the auditorium was her aura. It looked very muddy, with lots of brown and gray colors. When I read for someone, I am in tune with his or her aura. My guides help me to peel back the layers of the aura—much like peeling an onion—so that I can understand what is going on. We all have helpers in the spirit world. Some are personal guides like family and friends who have passed on; others are teachers and healers from the higher realms. Because I work directly with many people, certain guides assist me, depending on what is needed. Certain guides help to amplify the energy around me so that I can tune in to the higher frequency of spirit communication. One of my guides is quick to point out physical issues like back problems or stomach ailments of the person for whom I am reading. Another guide often shares its spiritual wisdom through me to uplift an audience. But sometimes, the emotional stress is so heavy and the person's energy is so tightly wound up that it takes a lot of energetic influence for information to get through. That's what's so amazing about the work I do.

When spirits come through with evidentiary facts that are known only to a bereaved person, he or she is usually shocked into reality. The idea that a loved one is actually communicating from another world amazes not only the person in question, but the rest of the audience as well.

"Can I speak to you?" I asked Stacey.

She looked at me. I could tell that she was in a state of grief and despair that was destroying her.

"A young man about eighteen years old is standing by your side. He is smiling."

"No, it can't be him. He can't be smiling."

"But he is smiling, and he wants me to tell you that he is happier now than he has ever been."

Stacey gave me a tortured look.

"He doesn't want you to be so upset. He is trying to help you, but he can't because you are so stuck. Do you understand what I mean?"

Stacey shook her head.

"Is your son's name Tony?"

Suddenly, she perked up. "Yes, that's his name."

"He was very athletic, wasn't he? He is showing me a skateboard or a snowboard. He loved all kinds of sports."

"Yes, that's Tony. He loved doing anything outdoors."

"Your son was a free spirit, but he didn't feel free inside his body. He was a daredevil because he wanted to feel alive all the time. He is saying that he is free now."

"I didn't know that he felt that way."

"He wants you to forgive yourself. You did nothing wrong. Do you understand? *You're not to blame,* he is saying."

"But I am to blame. I could have been a better mother. I could have seen the signs. I could have been there when he needed me the most."

"You can't control what happened to your son. He wants you to forgive him for putting you through such agony."

Stacey couldn't speak; her eyes filled with tears.

I listened to Tony some more and turned to her once again. "He is pleading with you to forgive yourself and him. He feels your pain and can't move on until he knows you are all right."

"I don't know if I can."

"He is telling me about a trip the family took. I see a winding road and a cabin. Now he is showing me people in the snow. You and he are having a snowball fight. He is laughing so hard at you because you keep falling down."

Stacey smiled for the first time.

"He wants you to stop the pills."

Stacey winced as a murmur of voices moved through the audience. She began to cry.

"I don't want to live without my Tony."

"Tony wants you to live. He wants you to get well so he can connect with you. He is saying your mind is cloudy and he can't connect. *Please, please,* he says. *I love you. Forgive me.*"

Stacey nodded her understanding. "Tell him I'll try."

Tony faded away.

When a person is blocked in grief and despair as Stacey was, even those from the spirit world have a hard time getting through with their healing energy.

Stacey took pills to numb her pain. But the pain couldn't go away if she would not face it, go through it, and release it. The downward spiral for a hopelessly grieving person establishes itself quickly. This kind of grief can also be a cry for help. Some people can feel very comfortable in their grief, because it becomes a reason for not doing anything else. That is why it is important for the grief-stricken to have the support of family and friends or become part of a group. Otherwise, overwhelming grief can lead to self-destruction. If you or someone you love is struggling with grief, your company is the greatest possible gift you have to offer and share.

Enrich Others

We have different belief systems, different levels of spiritual understanding, and different ways of coping. As with any situation, we can either grow stronger or be controlled by our circumstances and be afraid of them. I have met many parents who have lost children and, as they will tell you, it was the worst thing that could ever have happened to them. And yet their loss also offered many magical moments from which they learned and became better people. For some, the tragedy helped them find their spiritual path; for others, like Marie Levine, it was an opportunity to step into a fuller experience of life.

As I said earlier, everyone grieves differently, but there is always a positive benefit when one partner is empathetic and does not berate or blame, but rather supports and acknowl-edges, the other. Not all relationships have to fall apart. Yes, at first, life is turned upside down, but eventually, by allowing and understanding each other's grief, life begins to take on a whole new meaning. The feelings expressed bring greater depth to a relationship.

One of the first steps in a positive recovery for many couples is to live a life their child would be proud of. Even though the child may no longer be in the physical shell, it will watch its earthly parents from the heavenly world. Parents can con-tinue to teach their children how to handle various situations in positive ways. For instance, if a child was hit by a car at an intersection with no light, its parents can take up the cause and lobby to have a light installed, possibly saving many other lives. If a child died of disease, the parents can increase public awareness of the particular disease. Parents can also form sup-port groups to help other parents who have gone through the same experiences. We see these stories every day in the news. Parents can turn a tragedy into service and create positive out-comes for many others.

At the same time, it's necessary that parents serve them-selves. Parents must not neglect their own needs. Bereavement can devastate you physically as well as mentally. Parents need to make sure they remain healthy and physically active. Physi-cal fitness is a wonderful way to deal with stages of grief, be-cause exercise releases endorphins into the bloodstream—it is a natural feel-good remedy for the body.

Soul Pact

As part of its soul plan, each soul makes an agreement or a pact with other souls to learn particular lessons like humility or generosity, or to correct errors in judgment from past lifetimes, or to share love in a new way. These other souls are part of its soul group. Within a soul group are soul families and soul mates—a broad matrix of souls are involved in our earthly adventures. Members of a soul group can touch our lives for years, months, days, or merely moments. For instance, you may be at a party or a business conference and strike up a conversation with a stranger about something profound or close to your heart. Instinctively, you feel at ease with this person as if you have always known him or her all your life. Then, just as quickly, this person is gone, never to be seen or heard from again. This unexpected connection was preplanned at a soul level because there was something that you or the other person needed to hear or to say.

Soul pacts are agreements made in the spiritual realms before we incarnate into human form, and each soul involved must give its consent to take part. If you want to be more aware of your soul pacts, you must first become aware that you are souls on a spiritual journey. I have been asked countless times: How can I start to become aware that I am a soul? Or: How do I gain more of an awareness of the spiritual levels? I have one simple answer: Learn the art of mindfulness.

I once met a couple that had lost four children in less than ten years. I asked them how they had gotten through the pain of losing their children. I wanted to know if they had some secret formula that could help others cope. They explained that learning how to survive the loss was essentially a process of learning about themselves. "You can't shut yourself away or shut down how you feel," they told me. "You have to become aware of what is happening and realize that you can handle what you have been given. No one understands or knows you better than yourself."

This couple knew that they did not have all the answers to why they were in this situation. To better understand their circumstances and learn what they could do to ease the suffering, they began to meditate. In meditation, they learned how to let go of their busy ego minds and become mindful of being in the present moment. They became aware of their emotional reactions and how their grief was affecting their physical and mental well-being. They were able to acknowledge the reality of their losses and process each one in a positive way. They went through a lot of soul-searching with each death. I asked them how they could continue to have hope after each loss. They replied: "The pain of grief is just as valuable as the joy of love. It is a matter of putting it all in balance."

Here is their story.

I met Alice and Peter at a small demonstration I gave during one of my book signings. The couple, who were in their seventies, were sitting in the back of the room holding hands. I thought it was beautiful that, after many years in life, a couple their age still showed affection for each other. Nothing about them seemed special, except that I vividly recalled Alice's beautiful smile and bright energy. Her skin was soft and youthful despite her age. I had already given various messages to several people in the audience when I noticed the spirit of a young man standing behind Alice and Peter.

The spirit had brown hair and striking blue eyes, and appeared to be about twenty-five. As I stared over at him, he acknowledged me and telepathically sent me the name Joseph.

I turned to Alice and asked, "Do you know a Joseph, a young man who has passed?"

"Yes," she responded. "He was my son. He was just a baby when he died."

Suddenly, I thought I was seeing double. Another man who looked identical to Joseph stood on Alice's right and put his hand upon her shoulder.

"There is another man who looks just like Joseph. Does this make sense to you?"

In her very gentle demeanor, Alice answered, "Yes; that would be his twin brother, Joel. They both died shortly after birth."

"They are thanking you for coming tonight."

Often, when several spirits come together, they meld their thoughts and send me one cohesive message.

"The boy named Joel is telling me that you know very well that they are with you and help you every day. He is saying the word 'contrast.' Do you know what it means?"

"I do," exclaimed Peter. He laughed out loud, shaking his head.

"Joel is telling me that he and his brother were with you last Sunday when you were doing a crossword puzzle and you couldn't come up with that word."

Peter laughed again. "I couldn't figure it out, so I looked up to heaven and called to the boys, 'Hey guys, I need your help.' A few minutes later, the word 'contrast' came into my head. They talk to us all the time."

Then I became very aware of a woman named Betty standing to my left. She was asking me to thank her mother for volunteering.

"There is another spirit by the name of Betty. She wants to thank her mother for volunteering. Does this belong to anyone here?"

I looked around and no one responded.

Alice spoke up. "That must be my Betty. She died many years back. A few weeks ago, I started volunteering at an adoption agency to do a few errands."

As Alice spoke, I was thrown for a loop. Most of the time, I am the one who shocks others; rarely is it the other way around. As I was gathering my thoughts, Betty sent another message. I relayed it to Alice.

"Betty is saying to tell you that you're doing a perfect job with the pact your group planned out."

"Thank you, I appreciate that," responded Alice.

Suddenly, a person sitting along the aisle raised her hand. "What did she mean by that—about a group and a pact?"

"Let me ask Betty," I said.

Alice smiled knowingly as both sons placed their hands on their parents' shoulders.

Betty had already answered in my head, as if she had been anticipating the question. She fired off thoughts and explanations as if she were teaching a class in rudimentary spirituality. I verbalized exactly what I was hearing.

"She says that she, her parents, her brothers, and two other sisters are part of a soul group. This means that they have experienced many lifetimes together. They came back on this earth to learn together."

"Or in heaven," Alice interrupted.

I relayed to the audience the words Betty was spouting off in my head. *We each have to learn individual soul lessons that help the group to evolve as well. My lesson this time was about giving others the chance to demonstrate compassion and kindness to me.*

Curiosity got the better of me. I asked Betty how she died and she responded, *Leukemia.*

"She says she died of leukemia. Is that true?"

Alice and Peter nodded in the affirmative. "We took good care of her. She was a doll, always caring about everyone around her. She takes care of little children now."

"What do you mean?" I asked.

"Her job in heaven is to help little children cross over into the light. She waits for them on the other side so they won't be afraid."

The whole audience gasped in surprise—myself included.

Then I asked, "What were the lessons the rest of your group had to learn?"

As Betty's messages came to me, I caught sight of another spirit woman standing next to her. She spoke her name.

"Do you know a woman who passed named Jacqueline or Jackie?"

"Yes, that is our other daughter. She died in a car accident at age seventeen," Peter admitted.

I was stunned. I had to voice what everyone else must have been thinking.

"Alice, you lost four of your children?"

"Yes, I did. But, I never felt I lost them. I feel we are just in different parts of life. We are here doing what we have to, and they are there doing what they are meant to. I know one day we will see one another. All in good time."

I wasn't sure what amazed me more: the fact that there was an elderly couple who had lost four of their children or the fact that they were in very good health and seemed quite well adjusted. Theirs was an incredible lesson for all of us who had the great pleasure to be in their company.

I asked Alice and Peter to stay behind at the end of the event because I wanted to speak with them more. When we were alone, I expressed my gratitude for their attending the demonstration and sharing their amazing life story with everyone.

That is when Peter said, "Sure, that's our job!"

His wife added, "That is also part of our soul-group pact. We had to learn about abandonment, attachment, reality of life and death, and how the only true thing is love. We do everything out of love. We were pleased to be able to give our children the opportunities they needed to come back for as long as they needed. We were able to fulfill our obligations. What a joy."

I already had ideas swirling in my head about bringing this brilliant story to the public, because it was such a helpful and positive message about death, grief, and love. When I asked them if I could write about their message, Alice said, "That is why we came. We wanted to share our story, to let others know that death is just a doorway, to be mindful of yourself and others, and to learn not to take everything so seriously!"

I felt blessed.

Ten minutes later, as I was gathering my pens and the various items people had left for me on the book table, I looked up and saw Alice and Peter surrounded by their entire family joyfully walking out together into the cool night air.

2

A Child Arrives
in Spirit

Children are souls that kiss the earth.

—DORIS STOKES

A S HUMANS, WE HAVE a body, mind, and soul. When
we die, only the physical body dies; the mind and soul
remain alive and aware. Ageless and timeless, our
souls have inhabited this earth many times in many bodies. We
have also existed in other forms and manifestations on various solar systems, universes, and dimensions. Each particular
place provides a soul with specific lessons necessary for the
soul to evolve in a certain way at that time. We have an innate,
spiritual sense to learn and comprehend everything about life
in order to adapt, and we join with others, either as teachers
or students, to learn—for no one can fully comprehend life
without the assistance of others.

At the time of death, a soul returns home, perhaps after a
very long voyage on earth. It is different for a child. Because
a child has only briefly stopped on the shores of earth, when it

returns to its spiritual home base, the ways of the spirit world feel quite familiar and natural.

How and under what circumstances a child has left the physical body may suggest the conditions it will find on the other side. If, for instance, a child was seriously ill, it may awaken in a hospital setting. Here, the child will receive help to reenergize its energy life force, or *prana*, that was drained during the illness. Prana comes from ancient Sanskrit and means "vital life." It is prana that energizes and activates the soul back to health. I often use the analogy of prana being the gas that fills up the tank. It is interesting that, although I know this occurs, I rarely hear children speak of hospitals or long recoveries. Most children enter the other side easily and effortlessly, no matter the circumstances of death.

Let me just add that children very rarely remain earthbound as ghosts. Remember that children are not burdened by negative emotions like adults, although there are always exceptions. If a child is murdered, it may stay to help its parents find the killer. Or if a child is missing, it may stay to help locate the physical body and ease the parents' minds.

Parents always ask the question: Why? Why did this happen to us, to my baby, to our family? My answer, based on experience, is that no child dies before its time. When a soul has fulfilled its purpose in life, death comes. There is no such thing as an accident from a spiritual point of view. The transition is considered an important turning point in a soul's life plan. Furthermore, no child *ever* dies alone. The spirit world is well aware of each child's return to its heavenly home, and spirits wait in readiness for its arrival.

Usually, a child is met and guided to the other side by someone it knows—a grandparent, an aunt, or another significant soul connection. It may even be someone the child never knew in its recent lifetime—someone known in a previous lifetime. Or the child may be brought into the light by spirit helpers who have a special affection and love for children. These guides often choose to be emissaries to youngsters for a number of reasons: they did not or could not have children while on the earth, or they are experienced at raising children, or they are well-qualified caregivers. These spirit helpers act as foster parents, if you will, comforting newly arrived children.

No matter how a child dies, whether from a freak accident, an overdose of drugs, or a terminal illness, the first sense he or she has when leaving the body is one of freedom. Think of it as taking off a heavy overcoat in the heat of a summer's day. All discomfort, pain, and torment are gone. The vulnerability and perhaps helplessness they once felt on earth quickly fades away. A child enters the spirit world with a lot less emotional baggage than an adult. Instead, the spirit feels incredible joyfulness and an overwhelming sense of peace, as this next story demonstrates.

I'm Alive!

I was teaching a weekend workshop in California about the various techniques of mediumship. In order to make contact with a spirit, I have to establish a link and bring myself to a level of receptivity. I accomplish this through meditation. As mentioned, meditation clears away the space of ego and opens the necessary channels for spirits to influence my mind with their thoughts. Once the link is established, I demonstrate how to build the evidentiary information that a spirit communicates. In the midst of this particular demonstration, I had a surprise visitor from the spirit world.

As I concentrated on opening my mind to Spirit, my thoughts were filled with an image of a young boy around the age of nine. He was walking toward me. His name was Jeffrey.

I need to let my mom and dad know I am all right. I can't get through to them. My mom is always on my bed crying and she does not see or hear me.

As I said before, when humans are in such a crushing state of grief, it is difficult for spirits to get through. Only with the help of guides or other advanced spirits can they make the connection. As long as I have been doing this work, I have heard one message over and over from spirits: I'm not dead, but very much alive!

I asked Jeffrey, "How did you die?"

Jeffrey impressed me with his thoughts, telling me that he was at a lake. *I was fooling around on the top of a rock. I slipped and fell off and hit my head,* he said. *I'm sorry that I made everyone sad.* Then he told me that he wanted his parents not to be sad.

I turned to the people in the workshop. "Is there a link between someone here and Jeffrey?"

A woman raised her hand. "I think it might be my nephew. He died of a brain aneurysm after slipping off a rock!"

I asked Jeffrey, "Can you give me some more information, please?"

I listened to the young boy and turned back to the woman. "Jeffrey says that his Grandpa Jimmy was there."

The woman gasped. "Oh my god, that's him."

"He says that he wants his mother to be okay."

Jeffrey's aunt replied, "I will give her the message. She feels so guilty about not being able to save him. She feels it's all her fault."

I took the opportunity to ask young Jeffrey about his life in Spirit.

"What do you do over there?"

I go to school, same as before, he replied.

"What are you learning?"

Different stuff. I can do whatever I want. I like to make things with my hands, so I am learning to do that. My teachers help me a lot.

"Do you have friends your own age?"

Sure, he replied. *There are plenty of kids here, and we play and have fun.* He said that he could get around a lot faster than he could before. If he wants to go somewhere, he just has to think of it with his mind, and he's there. *I don't need my bike,* he told me. I passed all this along to my audience.

"Is there anything else you want to say?" I asked him.

Just tell Mommy and Daddy that I'm still alive, and I can see them all the time, he answered. I turned to Jeffrey's aunt and asked her if she understood.

She nodded.

When I looked at the rest of the audience, I could see several people crying. Jeffrey's childlike innocence and openness had permeated the entire room, and the joy of his energy had touched everyone.

Kylie's Tour of Heaven

As I was writing this chapter, Kylie, the little girl at the mortuary, suddenly appeared in my mind. As a medium, this trance-like state happens to me from time to time. Nonetheless, I was a bit surprised to see Kylie again. She immediately jumped on her white Shetland pony and began flying around.

Just then, another figure approached Kylie. He was dressed in a tan linen suit, and I quickly realized that he was Kylie's guide. Who are you? I asked. *I'm Herbert*, he replied. *I'm sort of like the Welcome Wagon here.*

Herbert and Kylie sat under a tree. Herbert spoke to Kylie, saying, *You will be going to school just as you did on earth.*

Kylie replied, *I want to learn to make beautiful clothes with all different colors so I can dress up my doll.*

The guide pointed to a breathtaking building decorated with mother-of-pearl and gold. Herbert added, *You might attend this one.*

Kylie stared at the array of colors emanating from the top of the building. Her guide further explained that designers in heaven often impress the minds of humans with their creations. That is how people on earth get ideas to make new things. Kylie asked, *You mean clothes are made in heaven first?*

Her guide patted her hand. *Everything—paintings, stories, music, and science—are all created in heaven before they make their way down to earth.*

Kylie then asked, *Why do people have so many different colors?*

Herbert explained that colors define who they are as souls. Certain colors present a soul's level of understanding and maturity. Other colors show a soul's level of interest. For example, a soul who is a carpenter may show red, revealing his strength.

As Kylie and Herbert toured what appeared to be an incredibly luminous landscape, I heard Kylie remark, *It's like Disneyland. All the beautiful lights. Tinker Bell must be touching everything with her magic wand.* Then she asked her guide, *What do people do here?*

Herbert beamed with delight and replied, *Whatever is in their hearts that they desire.* He pointed to a person playing the piano. *That man always wanted to do that on earth,* he said. *He's finally taking the proper lessons.* Then he showed a person painting on a large canvas and told Kylie that there are great masters in the spirit world who teach art and music. These souls have been creative throughout many lifetimes.

As they walked up a small green slope, a group of children and adults seemed to be having a picnic. It reminded me of a festive Easter Sunday outing. No one seemed to be in a hurry. I could see a huge stone building in what appeared to be a Roman plaza, complete with a towering, ornate marble fountain.

Where are we? Kylie asked.

Herbert answered, telling her that this was one of the many Halls of Reception, where family and friends gather to greet the new arrivals. Kylie ran to play with the children in what looked like a beautiful park.

Herbert continued to communicate with me. *It's a very happy place. Everyday there are thousands of reunions. Those who thought they were dead wake up to see they are very much alive, and that they have arrived home.* Herbert then escorted Kylie to a couple whom the little girl immediately recognized. At that moment, my trance ended. I wondered if the couple were Kylie's grandparents or some relatives from the past. She seemed very happy to see them.

My visit with Kylie and Herbert inspired me. I had had a glimpse of heaven before, but this tour was exceptional and I felt convinced that both Kylie and Herbert wanted me to share it in this book. I will now take you further inside this spectacular dimension.

The Spirit World

I already knew much of what Kylie showed me from thousands of readings and information given to me by my guides. Spirits first enter a sphere closest to the earth's dimension, known to many as the astral world. This is a level that very much resembles earth, with beautiful gardens, homes, forests, and lakes. The astral world incorporates all the beauty of the earth, but is much more vivid in color and aliveness. The astral dimension is a world without time, so there is no day or night. Although there appears to be a sun, the illumination of this world actually comes from the incandescent beauty of its surroundings. All is lit from within, not from an outer orb.

It's understandable that a little girl like Kylie would think of the astral world as Disneyland, with Tinker Bell waving a magic wand. As adults, we might imagine it as a world viewed through 3-D glasses—only without the glasses. For instance, we would see buildings from every angle simultaneously. Every structure would seem to vibrate with the energy of those who created it and would be in perfect harmony with its environment—sparkling and shining, spacious and welcoming.

Spirits often speak about the spirit world as a magical kaleidoscope filled with rich and vivid colors. Spirits not only see color; they also feel color. Colors not only seem alive to them, they also communicate specific qualities. As Herbert inferred, red communicates power and vitality. Blue translates into tranquillity and fluidity; green indicates healing and caring; yellow represents intellectual acuity, and so forth. When spirits of children appear to me, their colors are beautifully bright; they have not had enough time in their earthly lives to be contaminated by the darker energies of judgment and lack.

Because senses are heightened and alert in the spirit world, communication is also vastly different there. On earth, we have to use computers and cell phones to communicate. In Spirit, every idea is exchanged through thought. As soon as a spirit thinks, its thought is manifested and becomes a reality! This can be a double-edged sword for spirits still bogged down in negative human emotion. If whatever they are thinking manifests, every spirit around them can see and feel what they are thinking.

Most of my work is done through thought and feeling. I am able to connect to departed souls in much the same way souls communicate with one another in Spirit. It is quite liberating, because the information comes instantly—there is nothing to remember or forget.

As Herbert described, when children arrive, they are greeted by a guide in the Hall of Reception. From there, they visit an open arena to receive a cleansing of earthly emotional patterns acquired during their sojourn on earth. Rarely do children have negative energies of their own. Depending on their previous earthly environment—whether it was nurturing and happy, or depressing and restricted—any negative energy that attaches to them is from the beliefs of their parents, relatives, teachers, and friends. So when children enter the open arena, a shower of light energy washes over them, cleansing any unwanted energy that may have stuck to them on earth.

My Soul Is Clean

While I was doing a demonstration in Atlantic City several years ago, a teenage girl came through with a remarkable story that I would like to share with you.

I began the demonstration with my usual opening statements about myself and how spirits contact the living. After my short spiel, I proceeded to close my eyes, said a short prayer, and asked for my spirit guides to help and protect all in attendance. When I opened my eyes, I immediately saw a figure waving at me. At first, I thought it was a very short woman, but as I approached the back of the auditorium, I realized that it was a young girl around fifteen years old. She looked quite fragile, yet attractive, with long, dark hair and deep-set brown eyes. She was smiling and waving and, as I moved closer to a group of women in the audience, she began pointing at them with great enthusiasm.

I turned to the three women in front of me and said, "I have a teenager here who is very determined to talk to you."

The women's eyes lit up and one of them began to cry.

"Who is Gemma or Jenna?"

"Gina!" they exclaimed in unison.

I smiled at this group's excitement. Gina began showing me her story.

"Gina is showing me a big crowd, like a party. There are a lot of young people dancing. It's packed with kids. I can feel a lot of energy—they are out of control, a lot of drinking going on. Most of these kids are drunk. Do you understand, please?"

"Yes," said one of the women.

"What is your name?" I asked the woman who had replied.

"I'm Denise, Gina's auntie." She turned to the other two women. "This is Pauli, Gina's sister, and Rita, her mother."

I touched my head. "I can feel something hot and burning in the back of my head." I kept looking at the scene Gina was communicating to me, and nodded my understanding of what was happening.

"Your daughter was shot in the head, wasn't she?" I asked Rita.

Rita's eyes began to fill with tears. "Yes, she was shot at a birthday party."

"I'm understanding that the person who shot her wasn't supposed to be there. Gina is saying that he crashed the party. He didn't belong there."

"Yes, he was looking for someone in a gang who was supposed to be there. He started to shoot at people. Gina was hit before she knew what was happening."

Pauli grabbed her mother's hand and squeezed it. Gina began showing me more of this terrible scene.

"There were a lot of drugs at this party," I relayed. "A lot of kids strung out. A lot of negative energy around them—dark energy."

"What do you mean?" Denise asked.

"Wherever there are a lot of drugs and alcohol and people out to do harm, there is always a lot negative energy—not only from the living, but also from the earthbound dead."

I looked at Rita. "Your daughter was caught up in the wrong crowd. There was anger and hatred there—a lot of darkness in that room. She was in the wrong place. Do you understand this?"

Pauli answered this time. "My sister liked a boy who was in a gang. I told her not to hang out with him, but she wouldn't listen. She always said, 'he's got my back.'"

Gina continued sending me messages. They were coming through so quickly that I had to ask her to slow down. When she paused, I passed her thoughts on to her three relatives.

"She says now she understands that her boyfriend was not so great. He was always dealing drugs, wanting more and more money, not caring whom he hurt. She is telling me that he always acted big and tough. She didn't know that he would kill anyone for a few bucks."

Rita was quietly listening, clutching Pauli's hand.

I started to explain to the rest of the audience. "This poor girl was caught in a very negative energy field. She hung around with kids who carried a lot of anger inside them. Our thoughts create our reality. If we live in fear and anger, we create that fear and anger in our lives. We pull what we are feeling to us. Gina attracted negative energy just by hanging around her boyfriend. She could have walked away, taken her sister's advice, but she didn't. It was a soul lesson for her. She thought she could overcome his negativity in some way. It was a very hard lesson."

Then I turned to Rita, Pauli, and Denise. "Gina was very naive in some respects. She wanted to believe in this boy, although she knew down deep that he was lying about the drugs and the fights."

They nodded their understanding.

"Gina is with her great-aunt and -uncle. They are taking care of her now."

Denise spoke up. "But she was only a child when they died."

"She says she knew them from going to church."

"That's right," said Rita. "They took her to church with them every Sunday."

"She says she was watching everyone at the funeral."

"Oh my god," gasped Pauli. "She was there?"

"She wanted to see all her friends again."

Gina sent another scene to my mind. "Gina says she had to get baptized again. Not the way it is done on earth, with water. She says she was baptized in light. She had to clear her mind of all the anger. She's sorry to cause you so much pain. She wants you to know that she's going to school now. She says she wants to help kids get out of gangs."

With that, Gina vanished from my sight.

When someone is cleansed in heaven, as Gina was, only the heavy earthly "poison" energies are cleared. Memories stay intact, and everything that we learn on earth remains with us. This cleansing is akin to waking from a restful night's sleep or a delightful dream, or coming out of deep meditation. We feel refreshed, clearheaded, and more aware of who we are. We no longer have the need to hold on to negative thoughts, harmful habits, or limited thinking—all of which was once associated with our earthly lives. We are finally free.

I've Grown Up

All children grow up in the spirit world, even babies. So when a child appears to its parents during a reading, it appears as a child they recognize. A child may also describe itself as the person it has grown into as an adult. Parents often recognize the traits of their children even as adults. For example, a spirit adult may explain that he or she is a musician, and the parents concur that the child had started taking piano lessons before it died. Parents are rarely surprised when told about their children's interests in the spirit world, as you will see from this following story.

A few years back, I did a demonstration in a Reno casino in front of a thousand people. I remember taking a sip of my coffee, turning to the audience, and saying, "I have a man and woman here. I believe they are connected in marriage." I pointed half-way back on the right of the room. "The woman used a walker before she died. She is giving me a name—something that sounds like Mathie or Mattie. Her husband is with her. The toe on his left foot was amputated due to diabetes. Does this make sense to someone?"

I scanned the auditorium. Finally, I heard a lady toward the back say, "Yes."

"Excuse me?" I said. "I really need to hear your voice in order to make the contact. Do you understand the information I just gave out?"

I noticed an overweight woman sitting on the right side of the room. She had a white bandana tied around her head. I could see that she was very apprehensive about standing. I must say this always amazes me. I understand being shy and not wanting to stand up in public, but the whole purpose of my events is to help people contact their loved ones. Many spirits do not get through because their loved ones don't stand up and participate. So if you attend my events, please take part.

After some coaxing, this middle-aged woman stood up. One of the runners passed her a microphone.

"Hi. What is your name please?"

"Roseanne."

"May I call you Rosie? That is what this man is insisting I call you, not Roseanne."

"That's my dad. He hated Roseanne and told everyone to call me Rosie!"

"Your mother is with him."

"Yes, her name is Mattie."

Rosie started to rock back and forth. I could tell she was very nervous. Her mother went on for quite a while.

"Your mother is saying that you need to clean out all the old boxes in the garage. She is also mentioning that there was a family of cats living among the boxes."

"I started to do it," she replied. "The cats are upstairs now."

Toward the middle of the communication, another spiritual being who seemed quite evolved stood between the mother and father. I was given a thought to convey to Rosie.

"Your parents are telling me that you are one of three children. Is that right?"

Rosie shook her head from side to side. "No, there's only me and my brother, Ben!"

"No, your mother is telling me you are one of three. Who is Gracie?"

At that moment, I thought Rosie was going to collapse. Thank God she brought her gambling buddies with her to hold her up.

"Oh, my God!" Rosie gasped and put her hands to her face.

"Do you know Gracie? Because she comes with your mother and father to say hello to you."

"Yes, yes, yes! Gracie is my twin sister. She died at birth. I survived, but she didn't." She broke down in tears. "I am so sorry, Gracie. I am so sorry."

"Gracie is quite happy and does not want you to feel guilty. That was not her soul's plan."

"What do you mean?" asked Rosie.

"She is telling me that you both have lived many lifetimes together and, in this one, you needed to learn more from the earth world than she did. She had to be where she had to be."

This was hard for Rosie to comprehend. I also think that this whole experience was a new kind of experience for her. I explained a little bit about soul groups and soul pacts.

Rosie interrupted. "Gracie died as an infant. Are you telling me she has grown up? Are you kidding me?"

"Yes, your sister has grown up in heaven."

Then Gracie took over my mind and, with the support of her lovely parents, began telling Rosie and the entire audience where she had been for the past forty years. The audience was buzzing.

"Gracie wants you to know spirits do grow up in the spirit world."

"How did she grow up?" Rosie was extremely curious about how this could happen.

"Your sister is telling me that she was with several guides. I can see her, and she is a lovely being."

Gracie filled me with thoughts and visions as quickly as I could receive them. "Your sister is telling me that, like all spirits who die young, she went to school. It was a school of her choice. She was very interested in the mind and how people behave, so she went into what here we would call psychology."

"Who are Aunt Dorie and Aunt Kaye?" I asked Rosie.

She turned white. "Those are my great-aunts. We never knew them."

"Well, they know Gracie. She has great love for her two aunts, who have guided her every step on the other side. She says they are very proud of her."

"What does she do over there?" Rosie questioned.

"Well, really whatever she wants."

I listened intently to what Gracie was sending me. "She has been trained to work with people on earth—particularly women who have a difficult time having children. She works with their emotional mind-set. She is saying that often they don't feel worthy. She tries to imbue into their earthly consciousness a sense of freedom from negative thoughts when it comes to pregnancy. She tells them to let God do the rest."

As I looked at the faces of the audience members, I could tell that, for many, this was the first time they had heard this kind of information.

Rosie had to sit down. She covered her face as tears flowed down onto the two little ripped tissues she was holding.

Gracie still had more to say. "Now she is showing me women giving birth. She says she helps the poor mothers and babies who die. She guides them into Spirit and stays with them until they adapt. *There are many things to do—lots to do*, she says. *It's important to have the freedom to express ourselves any way we choose.*"

Rosie was speechless.

I asked her, "How are you feeling?"

"I'm really freaking out!"

"Why?"

"James, do you know what kind of work I do? I am a counselor. I am also a midwife!"

This time, I was the one who was speechless.

There was an enormous hum in the audience. No wonder the two women were twins. Both had taken similar paths, only on different planes of existence.

Earthly parents can rest assured that their children are tended with great love and care in the heavenly spheres. When it is their time to pass, their children will be waiting for them. The children may first appear as parents remember them, but eventually, they will show how they have grown up. Each soul recognizes the other because of the deep bond that connects them. In the next chapter, I will discuss how a child occupies its time in the spiritual dimension while waiting for a loved one's return home.

3

A Child's Life in Spirit

For worry not what children do when
Heaven calls them home;
There are tasks and games and lessons, too;
many more than fits this poem.

—BRIAN RAY

SOUL NEVER STOPS GROWING and evolving no matter what form of life it takes. Sometimes a soul needs many years on this earth to understand its spiritual nature and will take on many challenges in order to know the fullness of its being. Sometimes a soul needs to touch the earth only briefly in order to complete its lessons and fulfill its soul pact with those in its soul group and soul family.

As Kylie described in the previous chapter, when children pass into the world of Spirit, their souls go directly to a realm of magnificent light made of glorious buildings, parks, waterways, and picturesque environments. It is also a place of intense soul-work, learning, and play. When children wake up in their heavenly home, they feel an innate stirring of familiarity because, like all souls, they have died and been reborn many times. While reestablishing themselves in their pleasant new home and getting reacquainted with their teachers, they have a great deal of help from other children, guides, family members, and those with whom they have shared a multitude of lifetimes. Kind and loving spirit helpers that first ushered them into the light continue to help them throughout this adjustment period.

Because the bond between parent and child is perhaps the strongest, it is only natural that a child may still desire to be with its earthly mother and father. Like all newly arrived souls, children can hear the prayers and thoughts of their still-embodied loved ones, and the cries of pain and sorrow can be especially difficult for them to bear. Because their senses are magnified, children are extremely vulnerable to the overwhelming grief of their earthly parents, which constantly pulls them toward the earth plane. The contrast between their earthly parents' suffering and their vividly beautiful, happy, and joyful spiritual environment can be a bit confusing.

This is a time when children's guides and spirit families are put to task. First, they must assist the young ones to adjust to their new home; then, it is vital that they escort them back to earth to be near their parents. This may sound intolerable, but it is not. Within a child's soul—indeed, within every soul—lies an awareness and knowledge of its limitless essence. In order to appreciate the entire scope of their situation fully, children must be able to bridge the gap between their new circumstances in Spirit and the love they still feel from those on earth. Like every soul trying to communicate with its earthly loved ones, a child will use various ways in order to connect, which I will explain later in the book. Suffice it to say that I have often seen spirits standing right next to their loved ones trying to comfort them, even shouting to let them know of their existence, but all communication is ignored. Because parents, especially, are in a whirlwind of shock, sadness, and confusion, children often feel at a loss when trying to make contact. The following story shows how a child attempts to ease its parents' grief.

My New Home

Bill and Jennie lost their son, Max, three years before I arrived at their cousin's home to do a reading. I could tell that they had been unable to move on from the pain of their loss. This was the first time Bill and Jennie had been to a psychic, and they were tentative at best. Bill, especially, was skeptical of my ability to contact his son. However, this did not last long.

"A little boy with blond hair and blue eyes is showing me the beach," I told them. "He is wearing a red bathing suit." The vision appeared very quickly and I shared it with Bill and Jennie.

"Yes, yes—that's right. Oh, my God!" Jennie said as she looked over at Bill, who was completely flabbergasted. Bill bent his head and rubbed his eyes.

"Your son is a good communicator. I am hearing his thoughts quite clearly. I can see him running around everywhere. He is showing me that you are yelling at him all the time to come to you, but he runs the other way!"

"Yes, all the time. He was always running away from me!" said Jennie.

Although amazed, the couple was still anxious. I did my best to reassure them. As further information came through, their doubts began to fade.

"He is showing me a calendar."

Jennie and Bill remained silent, as I listened for Max to continue.

"Did you go to the beach the first week of August? He is saying that his sister, Millie, was with him."

I could see Bill's face turn pale with surprise. "Yes, we went on vacation to Nantucket."

At this point, Bill and Jennie began to relax. Once they opened their energy to what was taking place, the communication with Max just flowed, and his thoughts started to fly around in my mind.

I explained to the couple what was happening. "It's as if there's a movie running across my mind. I can see everything Max wants me to see. Now he is playing in the sand. I can see him dump a bucket of sand as if he were building some kind of wall. He runs down to the surf and gets more sand, wet sand. Jennie, you are warning him not to go far."

At this point, I looked up and could see both parents crying. They confirmed that the events had occurred in just that way.

"He says that the last thing he heard was Jennie screaming Millie's name. I see Millie running and you chasing her. Suddenly, a huge wave crashes on top of him and drags him under the water!"

Bill squeezed his wife's hand.

I paused for a moment.

"He remembers that he couldn't breathe anymore and could see people on the beach running around. Bill, I can see you swimming out to him. He wonders why you don't realize it is too late. He has already stopped breathing. His body has hit a huge rock and his body floats facedown. He says, *I should have been more careful. I should have listened to you, Mommy.*"

Through her tears, Jennie interrupted me. "Oh my baby, was he afraid?"

"No, not at all. He says that he had a sense of being pulled up far above his body, and a warm feeling came over him. *As I looked over my shoulder,* he says, *I saw a big round golden light the color of butter.* He is looking at this light and feels only love. *I just want to go into the light,* he says. I see three beings in this light moving toward him. He says that he recognized two from the pictures on Mommy's dresser: One is the man with no hair."

"My grandfather," Jennie replies with a smile.

"I see a woman reaching out and grabbing his hand. She has deep-blue eyes."

"Oh, God—my mother!" Jennie cries out. "I asked her to help Max."

Max then showed me another person, and I gathered from this being's unique attire that he must be Max's guide. "He looks like a ship's captain with white hair and white beard, a white suit embellished with gold braiding, and a captain's hat. In fact, he looks a lot like Santa Claus without the red suit and sleigh. Max says that he feels love for this Captain Santa Claus person."

Bill breaks in. "Where did they take you, son? Where did you go?"

I tilted my head to hear Max's thoughts. "He is standing in front of a huge church, more like a cathedral. *But it's not a church,* he says. *It's a place where everyone meets each other.* It looks like a big hall. Now he is shouting: *Charlie is here!*"

I asked the parents, "Who's Charlie?"

Jennie laughs. They answer in unison: "His dog."

"He says the people were very nice to him. He is playing with Charlie and the other children in the garden. He says his friend is there—the one who got hit by a car.

"He sees Tommy Wavier," Jennie cried.

Then the tone of the conversation abruptly switched. Max started spouting off a checklist.

"He is showing me something else. Bill, did your cell phone go dead right after Max's death."

Bill took a moment to think back. "Yes, that's right. My phone didn't work the next day. I called the phone company, but they said I still had a connection."

"Max is saying, *It was me! It was me!*"

"Did you see the lights flicker on and off in his bedroom?"

"Yes! That happens a lot," answered Jennie.

"That's your son!" I had a big grin on my face. "He says he comes to see you with his teachers to let you know he is fine. *Don't cry, Mommy. Don't cry. It makes me very sad to see you cry.* He wants you to know that he is very much alive and living in a beautiful place. *I'm in heaven,* he says. He mentions that he will come to you in your dreams when your minds are open and not filled with sadness. The sadness covers your minds like a blanket, and he can't get through to you."

"I understand," responded Jennie. "We just miss you so much, Max," she cried.

"Bill, he remembers the first time you took him on a boat. He says he loved it. Did you buy him a sailor's cap?"

"It was a captain's hat. He told me that he had one just like it once. I had no idea what he was talking about and didn't pay much attention to it."

"He wants you to know that this is not the first time he died in the ocean."

Jennie let out a gasp.

"Why did he leave us?" Bill wanted to know.

"He says that his soul had experienced many lives at sea, and he has always been drawn to it. He says he came to be in the sea again. He was not afraid of the ocean. He doesn't want you to be afraid. *Don't be afraid,* he is saying."

I could feel a sense of relief in Jennie and Bill, and the energy in the room seemed a lot lighter.

"What is he doing now?" Bill asked.

"He is saying that he watches over his sister from heaven. *I will take care of her,* he promises."

Jennie almost began to cry again.

"He is going to school now."

"What are you studying?" Bill asked.

Max came back with an unforgettable answer. *Sea mammals. I want to understand the patterns of their thoughts.*

With this last word from Max, I knew that he was indeed a wise soul that had evolved far beyond the personality of a ten-year-old boy.

When I left Jennie and Bill, they seemed a bit more hopeful. I felt that Max's beautiful energy had been able to heal their broken hearts, and I hoped that they would be able to take the necessary steps to move on with their lives.

Spirit Schools

When children enter the heavenly sphere, they continue their education, as Max so eagerly revealed. Education in the spirit world goes far beyond earthly standards, as it is more creative and high-minded. Subjects are designed to align perfectly with each soul's spiritual make-up, intellect, creative talents, interests, and needs. Schools have not only teachers with a desire to bestow their knowledge and help children to blossom, but also master teachers from the higher spiritual spheres that teach more advanced subjects. These master teachers also help those souls planning to become teachers on earth.

Subjects run the gamut from earthly creativity to spiritual concepts. A music student, for example, will not only learn all facets of music composition and instrumentation, but also learn the emotional aspect of how music can elevate awareness and inspire imaginations. The same is true for schools where painting, sculpture, architecture, and design are taught. There, students learn not only the meaning and value of color and form, but also how to create in the most aesthetically pleasing and harmonious way. For the technically minded, education encompasses everything from engineering to technology, and mathematics to medicine. Scientists have laboratories in which to do their research. Many a new invention and scientific concept began its life in these spiritual schools and was then passed into the earthly realm via telepathy.

Spiritual schools do not have the overcrowded classrooms we have here on earth, with many students fighting for the instructor's attention. On the contrary, each student is given optimum attention and encouragement to develop the skills, talents, and knowledge necessary to fulfill his or her highest aspirations. Each class is designed specifically to resonate with a student's temperament and level of understanding. Therefore, students are shown situations that cultivate positive character development and altruistic desires.

Even though, as I've said, souls continue to study subjects they studied on earth, they can always learn something new and different. Usually, souls have a calling for their particular area of learning and, with each incarnation, can progress further in their area of expertise. Many people who walk the earth now, and contribute to our world in a positive and productive way, more than likely died as children in other lifetimes. The time they spent in spiritual schools did much to refine their soul awareness and prepare them for future incarnations on the earth.

Children's Activities

Besides attending school, children entertain themselves with a wide range of activities like sports, games, and handicrafts. They enjoy swimming, cycling, gardening, baseball, wood carving, sailing, and anything else they desire. Some join a band, while others rehearse plays in a theater. They go to parties, attend concerts, visit museums, and on and on. They also spend their time studying in libraries or going to specialized lectures. Some become members of organizations similar to the Boy Scouts and Girl Scouts that teach leadership skills, teamwork, arts and crafts, conservation, and camping. Many spend their time in the animal world, taking caring of animals that have passed over. Children easily attune to animals and will visit animals on earth that are in need of help.

Rarely is a child by itself, because there are such a wide variety of social activities to keep children busy. Remember that, in the spirit world, everything happens through thought, and children can happily and simply move from one activity to another. Guides are always around to help them maintain a balance between school and social activities.

Assisting people on earth is one of the main activities in which children participate, and they usually travel in groups when they return to the earthly dimension. I will never forget the time two teen spirits showed up during one of my demonstrations in Los Angeles. It sticks in my mind because one of them always used the expression "Dude"— *Dude, we're okay*, or *Dude, we're sorry*. Both boys appeared simultaneously near their family members at opposite ends of the room. They explained that they had each died in a car crash after having binged all night on alcohol and ecstasy. What made their visit extraordinary was their desire to help one of the boys' cousins who was in the audience to give up alcohol and get into a program.

Over the years, I have seen bands of children around people. I remember asking a young female spirit why they were hanging around in groups. Her reply was very matter-of-fact: *Our job is to bring happiness and joy to unhappy souls by lifting the energy around them. All of us have come from families where we were lonely at times, so we know what that feels like, and we want to help souls feel better.* A very interesting insight, I thought, and it was not the last time I heard it.

Butterflies Are Free

I was giving a demonstration in Youngstown, Ohio. Although I had been to Ohio a few times on book tours, I had never been to this particular venue. As I often say, each city is very different and audiences often reflect that. Since this was my first time in Youngstown, I thought it would be quite interesting to observe the variety of circumstances in which spirits manifested. During the first half of the readings, I conveyed all sorts of messages to loved ones: a mother of two who died on the operating table after a simple surgical procedure went wrong; a husband who fell off a roof while changing gutters. I am always astounded by the amount of healing and closure the messages provide, not only for the immediate family, but for the entire audience as well. This next reading was one of those healing messages.

"I have a young boy here—actually several young boys. This boy is showing me a hospital room. Now I am seeing a calendar with March 7th circled. He is saying he died on his birthday!" Just then, I touched my right side. "He died of appendicitis. Does this make sense to anyone in the audience?"

I looked around the room and saw a blonde-haired woman stand up. A girl of about ten and a boy about twelve stood up alongside her.

"That's my brother," spoke the ten-year-old. Her mother nodded her head in agreement.

"He is telling me that he would have celebrated his eighth birthday. Is that right?"

"Yes," said the mother. "He had just had his cake and ice cream that night, and woke up early the next morning complaining about a bellyache."

"Who is Tim?"

"That was his name. Timmy," said his brother.

"He wants me to let you know he has met Old Man Stebbins."

The three of them let out a mutual, "Wow!" Timmy's sister turned and whispered something in her brother's ear.

"Is there something else?" I asked.

"That is just so weird, because Timmy died a week after Mr. Stebbins, and we wondered if they had seen each other. They were pretty close."

"Timmy shows me butterflies pinned to a mat and framed like a picture. You know—like the ones you see in a science class."

"Yes, yes!" cried Tim's mother. "Mr. Stebbins gave Timmy his butterflies. They were his prized collection. He used to tell Timmy war stories about Vietnam. He was very depressed after his wife died. Timmy always tried to cheer him up."

"Who is Helen or Ellen?" I asked.

"That was Mr. Stebbins's wife, Helen," answered Tim's mother.

I was aware of the young boy showing me a ceremony. "Timmy is showing me what looks like a Boy Scout ceremony."

I asked Tim's brother, "Do you know anything about a badge from the Boy Scouts?"

The whole family gasped. I was aware of Timmy placing his arm around his brother's shoulders.

Tim's brother wiped a tear from his eye. "Yeah. I got my merit badge last week."

"Your brother is telling me he was with you. He tells me you taught him how to tie knots."

"Yes. We did that a lot."

"He says, *Thanks Tom*. Is Tom your name?"

He nodded.

The mother then asked, "Can you ask him what he does now? I think I feel him a lot around the house."

I listened for Timmy's answer. He immediately showered my mind with images.

"He keeps busy with lots of things. He loves insects and nature. He is showing me a lecture hall like the ones in a university where he goes to study. Now he is showing me butterflies flying all around. He is shouting: *They are alive!*"

"He loved all sorts of insects," Tim's mother reported.

I asked Timmy about the other spirit children that I could see around him. *We're on a mission*, he says. *We go together to various places all over the earth and bring thoughts and feelings of joy and happiness to people to help them feel good.*"

"Sort of like goodwill ambassadors," I added.

"That's so interesting," remarked Tim's sister, "because a few weeks before he died, he was on his bed showing me his map of the world. He told me that he was going to go to all these places. I thought he was dreaming."

"Your brother is an evolved soul, like most children who pass on."

"That he was," his mother breathed.

"He is saying that you have something of his in your bag. *Open your bag,* he says."

The woman reached under her seat to grab her purse. When she opened it, something flew out. It looked like a butterfly. It could have been a moth.

People nearby let out a gasp.

"That's only Tim making himself known," I said. "He's pretty darn smart, isn't he?"

Life Review and the Council of the Wise

Upon arriving at the new side of life, a soul—whether a child, teenager, or adult—meets with what is commonly referred to as a Council of Elders. These are evolved beings—guides and teachers—who understand a soul's make-up, desires, and gifts, some of which are yet to be recognized. Even if young children have not spent a lot of time walking upon the earth, the Council reviews with them the days of their earthly sojourn. Babies and toddlers spend their time in nurseries. These angel children only meet the Council for review and preparation for their next lifetime. I will discuss this further in the next section, where we'll talk about preparation for return.

It is very important to remember that, although the soul's most recent personality was that of a child, it has been around for many lifetimes. Usually only an evolved soul will use a child's short life for its growth. No matter, each soul's most recent visit to earth was very necessary and planned, and it fulfilled its special needs or that of its soul group. At this point, a soul will evaluate its recent experiences and progress. The meeting with the Council focuses on a soul's life review. Did the soul accomplish what it set out to do? Did it fulfill its soul contract? A soul contract is similar to a soul pact. The difference is that a soul contract involves fewer souls—two, maybe three—it is a more tight-knit arrangement. As with a soul pact, each soul must consent to be involved. Did the soul learn its lessons of worth and love or will it have to be retested on these values in another lifetime? The review is methodical—there is never a need to rush in the spirit world, as there is no time.

In evaluating a child's life, consideration is always given to the fact that a child has fewer opportunities to experience and is not a fully formed personality. Even so, some spirits only need to go through the experience of birth in order to give other souls the experience necessary for their growth. The Council also considers a soul's service to others. Did it provide the necessary opportunities for others to love and serve? Did the soul learn from these opportunities as well?

Because I grew up a Catholic, I was taught that there was a Judgment Day on which it would be decided whether we went to heaven or hell. I let go of these beliefs as a young man and, through my work, came to understand the meaning of judgment and life review. Life review is an educational and enlightening process. The only judgment is our own, but because we are in the light of heaven, this judgment is tempered with grace.

A life review can be seen in a variety of ways. Some souls see their lives pass as if they were watching a movie. Others see scenes from their lives like episodic TV. Others see their lives in 3-D or as holograms. Some say they can see their whole lives in one big panoramic overview. Others say the scenes move quickly; some say they stop and start; some say they can zoom in on certain events. When viewing our lives, it is impossible to lie to ourselves. Life review is not about fault-finding or punishment. Our mistakes are tools from which we learn about self-worth and self-love. The smallest act of kindness toward someone is much more key to our evolution than any awards, material goods, or money we may obtain. In fact, earthly possessions are of no consequence in a life review.

As I have said, nothing is hidden in Spirit, not even the secrets we have kept. All of our thoughts, words, and actions are exposed, along with the motives and intentions behind them. If we were spiteful or hurtful to someone, we will feel our own vindictiveness. If we squandered opportunities because of arrogance and pride, we will feel our own self-destruction. Even our treatment of animals and plants will be shown. Nothing goes unnoticed during a life review. For some, a life review may feel like hell. But for most people who have led good, helpful, and honest lives, a life review will be rewarding. We are always where we are supposed to be in the cycle of life. Although, as humans, we forget our spiritual inheritance, our souls never forget.

I Am Finally at Peace

I found the following life review quite interesting, especially because of the circumstances surrounding the human death. I remember feeling a bit tired after finishing my meditation in the backstage dressing room of a theater in which I was appearing. I had already completed several readings during the first hour and was trying to psych myself up for the second half of the evening, as there would probably be another hour's worth of messages. As I was contemplating my timing, my mind was interrupted by the thought of a very young man named Teddy. Teddy kept giving me his name over and over, so I wrote it down on a piece of paper to remember it. I asked how he had died and he showed me a rope. He kept saying, *Please Mister, it is important you tell people about my death. It will help not only them, but me here as well. Please!* I mentally replied, Okay, fine, I'll help you right after the break is over.

Several minutes later, I was back on stage rubbing my hands, preparing to blend my mind with Spirit. I asked the young man to come through and make himself known. I was well aware of a number of spirits around me, all vying for my attention. I asked my guides to sort it out and let Teddy come through first. Teddy stood in front of me and put a rope around his neck.

"I have a young man here in front of me. His name is Teddy and he's about eighteen or nineteen years old. He hung himself, and it looks as if he did this on some sort of fire escape. He is a thin boy and wears glasses. Some may have called him a nerd."

Suddenly a cry came from a woman and man in the audience: "Oh, that's us!"

I looked in the direction of the voices. One of the stage assistants ran up to the woman and handed her a microphone.

"That's my boy, Teddy." The medium-sized woman and oversized man stood up. Both were shaking. The lady pulled a picture from her handbag and handed it to the runner, who rushed to give it to me on stage. I looked at it and, sure enough, it resembled the spirit Teddy standing in front of me.

"He is telling me that he was made fun of a lot. He was harassed. Who is Kenny?" I asked.

Both parents stumbled to answer: "That's the boy who beat him up."

"Teddy shows me a computer screen. Do you know about Kenny and e-mails?"

The mother started crying. Teddy's father answered. "Yes. Kenny wrote horrible e-mails to Teddy and also sent them out to everyone at school. He accused our boy of coming on to him."

I was shocked and upset at the same time. I thought to myself how horrific that was. Keep in mind that, when I am giving a message, I am communicating with a spirit as well as the loved ones in the audience. I could not help but feel sorry for this young boy. I told him so in my thoughts. He was a very decent kid, too, which made his death all the more terrible.

"He is telling me to say the names Ed and Darla."

"Those are our names," said the father.

"Did he want to be a teacher? I keep seeing him teaching others in a white lab coat."

"Yes. He wanted to major in chemistry and teach at a college," Ed replied.

Then Teddy filled my head with an incredible picture that I had to share with the audience. It was awe-inspiring and indescribable at the same time.

"You know, your son wants me to tell you something important. He shows me that he is sitting in a meeting room or conference room. It almost looks as if he is speaking with faculty members, but he informs me that they are his guides. He says that they talk about his life plan. He says that, even though you may not understand it, there was a purpose for his death. The soul goes back and forth for many reasons. Sometimes we die young; sometimes we die old. Some leave by disease, accidents, and natural causes; others depart through suicide. He is telling me that he has found nothing but love where he is.

He says everyone is born for the happiness of others. He does not hold anyone responsible for his death. It was part of his soul's plan. He is telling me that he had experienced ridicule in previous lifetimes, and he had always let it get the best of him. He was determined to grow a sense of self-love in this lifetime. During his life review, he witnessed all the times in this life where he had opportunities to love himself and change his soul's usual pattern, but he did not."

At this point, the whole auditorium was still.

"But he was a good boy," said Darla.

Just then, a spelling bee popped into my mind. I looked at Teddy's parents and asked, "Was he in a spelling bee?"

"Yes," said Darla. "In junior high. He won it! He was the champion of five divisions!"

"He tells me that he won a lot of medals and trophies for a lot of different things."

The parents nodded in agreement.

"These were opportunities to acknowledge his abilities, but he failed to accept his own worth."

Both parents brushed tears from their eyes.

"He wants me to tell you that he was not punished for taking his life. He didn't go to hell. He has to work on this aspect of his soul. He will have another opportunity to learn self-worth. He is saying: *My guides are working with me.*"

"We love you, Son. You will always be a champion to us!" declared Teddy's dad.

"He wants to thank you both for sharing lifetimes with him. He thanks you for your support and love, which mean so much. He is telling me that your love is what made him feel good about himself. He didn't realize it until he left this life and reached the light. *Thank you, thank you,* he says."

I started to cry myself. I sent my love to Teddy for all the people he had healed with his message.

Every soul has a plan, although it may not make sense to our limited mind-set. On the other hand, if there is no "death" and we come back for soul experiences, it makes sense that each soul will try many different settings and circumstances to demonstrate love, compassion, understanding, and service. There are many reasons we choose to live and die, and all are for our spiritual growth and the growth of the many souls with whom we share life. A soul's short life on earth can only accelerate its growth. No matter where we are in our spiritual evolution, we are where we are supposed to be, as you will learn in Part Two.

The Soul's Make-Up

4

The Soul

*. . . the Soul has existed for ages, working its
way up through innumerable forms,
from lower to higher—always progressing,
always unfolding.*

—YOGI RAMACHARAKA

THROUGH THE BREADTH and scope of existence, the essence of your being has traveled, gathering experiences of every human emotion, situation, nationality, race, gender, and type of death and birth. This indefinable essence, which has traveled across time, is a vast storehouse of unlimited knowledge and possibilities contained in a collection of memories that are locked deep inside you. What exactly is this pearl of great price? It is your soul.

Over the years, I have received many messages from Spirit describing the nature of the soul. Descriptions range from it being the nucleus of our being, to the power within, to the core of freedom. Scientists, metaphysicians, and psychologists have referred to the soul as the "super conscious." I know it as the source of all intelligent energy wherein our true selves reside. Only a thin veil of human amnesia hides our own truth from us.

The soul exists on many different levels of consciousness. It can be present on the physical plane and coexist on another dimension simultaneously. The soul is not human; therefore it does not possess human chemistry. However, it is colored by an accumulation of human lifetimes. The soul is always evolving, growing, and expanding based on the choices we make during the situations that come upon us.

The soul is not the same as spirit. These two concepts are distinctly different. The spirit is the ethereal counterpart of the physical body—our etheric body—whereas the soul is our entire essence. Spiritual power emanates from the soul. When we are in "soul consciousness," and live with soul awareness, we break through the illusions of the five senses and know true self-worth. As a result, we discover our "soul power." This power gives inspiration, beauty, peace, joy, and harmony to each and every moment of life.

Early in my psychic development, I asked Spirit to show me what a soul looked like. The answer came quite unexpectedly, like a bolt from the blue. I stepped onto a stage one evening, looking at the audience and expecting the usual view of auras, but I was pleasantly surprised. Instead, Spirit gave me the gift of seeing every person in the audience from his or her distinct soul level. Above each person's head was a colorful hue of otherworldly effervescence that I perceived as the individual's soul. This sight was very different from what I was used to seeing when observing auras. I describe it simply as a sea of diamonds. Moreover, like diamonds, some souls shone brilliantly while others lacked a certain sparkle. The slightest dullness could only stem from that person's own self-imposed fears and limitations acquired from erroneous belief systems.

To confirm that Spirit had given me this glimpse of the soul, I did an experiment with the audience. I guided them through a self-empowering meditation and asked them to recognize the inspiring, dynamic, and carefree soul within. I waited to see if the diamonds changed in any way. It was quite amazing to witness the difference from the start of the meditation to its finish. At the end, not only were the souls/diamonds shining more brightly, they seemed to expand beyond the room. At the same time, the colors blended together, enhancing the whole atmosphere. Someone entering the room at that very moment could not help but have felt the intense serenity, love, and energy all around.

Soul Personality

Although we are all, of course, connected to each other and to the world of Spirit, we each have a distinct personality that has been reworked, redesigned, and perfected through eons of living life upon the earthly plane. This unique personality has a natural tendency to attract things it likes, and to repel or disregard situations that are of little interest to it. Such personality tendencies are important, because they cause certain circumstances to occur. As the personality accumulates experiences, it learns and matures. To understand our souls, we must begin to uncover this personality and appreciate the beautiful mosaic that makes each of us who we are.

Although a soul is consciousness, this consciousness is far beyond anything we can fathom with a human brain. Like a human fingerprint, each soul has a unique identity that is shaped by color, light, and electromagnetic vibration. Souls are very versatile; they can live in human or alien forms, on the planet earth or in other galaxies, and they can assume any shape they wish. Soul personalities can and do express humor, intelligence, stamina, peacefulness, and other characteristics.

A soul that incarnates in human form chooses a certain physical body for reasons that have to do with its soul pattern and soul growth. It chooses certain proclivities—say, a body with certain brain chemistry, emotional capacity, and physical ability or disability. Souls choose bodies that will accommodate the work necessary to learn every facet of morality and behavior of the human experience. Some souls need all of their vibrancy and energy when entering the earth's dimension. For instance, a doctor in a third-world country may bring all his or her soul vibrancy to earth to tackle difficult and dangerous situations. Healers and other rescuers of the planet usually bring their entire soul energy to accomplish their souls' task. Other souls may only need a portion of their soul energy, because the particular lifetime is not very complicated or intense. Each soul chooses the perfect body necessary to achieve its goals. This idea can be reassuring for all of us—knowing that our bodies are the perfect ones for our souls.

Soul Fragmentation

The soul has an innate instinct to protect itself. At times of life-threatening trauma, violence, or danger, an aspect or part of the soul may leave the physical body and return to the source of all. This splitting-off is called "soul fragmentation." The part that leaves is sometimes referred to as "the wound that never heals." It is this absent part that many people search for in order to feel whole once again. Soul fragmentation can happen in physical or emotional circumstances like accidents, surgery, abuse, stress, rape, suicide attempts, shock, divorce, or situations of war. Other causes of soul fragmentation may occur when we are in situations in which we cannot forgive another person, or when we wish things were different and we can't change them. In these instances, we get stuck and leave a part of our soul energy with that situation. Whenever a part of our soul is left behind in a situation or relationship, we feel a separation, even though, on a conscious level, we may never understand why. The symptoms of soul fragmentation can include feelings of emptiness, depression, sleeplessness, isolation, or anxiety. Sometimes, the splintered aspects return to the soul, but we may never feel completely whole again.

Soul Pattern

As souls incarnating into human bodies, we develop certain mental and emotional patterns. To each incarnation, we bring lifetimes of experiences, behaviors, and decisions. Soul patterns can be so ingrained within us that, if a soul does not have a strong sense of self, it may fall back into bad habits. Many times, souls that have been obsessed with certain behavior patterns that have occurred repeatedly will participate in comparable situations to test themselves and to change the pattern. Often, the pattern to be changed is negative or destructive in nature, like feelings of abandonment, hurt, resentment, anger, or dissatisfaction.

For example, a soul that may want to learn humility to overcome lifetimes of arrogance and pride may place itself in a situation involving power and wealth. Because each soul has free will, even though a soul comes to earth to eliminate a pattern, it may become distracted or misguided, allowing the pattern to take hold once again. When the soul returns to Spirit, it will review the pattern with its guides and get the necessary help to strengthen its energy so that it can try again in another lifetime.

I am often asked about souls who do evil in the world. Souls who hurt other living beings are not highly evolved. The evil pattern, once created, may become a destructive obsession that is repeated lifetime after lifetime. A soul may want to overcome its destructive pattern, but may not have enough energy to do so. Therefore, it continues to fall into lives filled with negativity and evil behavior. These souls can become extremely damaged—so much so that special master healers are called in to retrieve, reform, and make whole the damaged energy. These souls remain isolated in Spirit until restoration is achieved.

Breaking a Soul Pattern

The following reading demonstrates a situation of pattern repetition. I have received many messages regarding this common occurrence in people's lives. I remember this particular evening very well. Before the event started, I was meditating in my dressing room backstage. Suddenly, a sixteen-year-old boy named Josh manifested in front of me. He was strong-willed and quite agitated. In my head, I heard: *I have to get a message through to my sister.* The sense I got from this young man was one of desperation. He communicated that he had pretty much screwed up his life and, by getting a message to his sister, he would be doing the one positive thing that could help him and her at the same time.

When the time came for me to begin the message portion of the event, I mentally asked Josh to blend his thoughts with mine. He appeared on my right side and pulled my energy toward the back of the room.

"I have a young man here about sixteen years old who is desperate to talk to his sister." I pointed to the right side. "She is sitting in this part of the auditorium."

Suddenly, a dark-haired girl shot up from her seat and called out, "That's my brother Josh."

I couldn't help but notice the pink streak in her hair. "Thank you," I smiled. Josh then began to impress the scene of his death in my mind. "He is showing me a hypodermic needle. He is sprawled out on the front seat of a car. He says he was standing next to the paramedics when they took his body from the car. Do you understand?"

The girl let out a heart-wrenching cry. "Oh, my God! Yes, that is right. It was the car I bought him. I should have never given him that car. I just knew that he would screw it up. If he hadn't had that car, he might still be alive today! I am so sorry, Josh." The girl began to cry.

"Your brother is saying, *It's not your fault*. He says it was his fault. He is telling me you bought him that car out of love. You must understand the intent behind the act was one of love. That is the greatest deed one can do for another."

She nodded. "Yes, I know." Tears streamed down her face. "I had to take care of him."

Then Josh did something that I have rarely experienced in all the years I had been doing this work. The best way to describe it is that he took me on a tour of his soul journey and I experienced it in my mind. I witnessed and felt things as if I were Josh. I went into a light trance as I described my experience to the audience.

"I am sitting in a beautiful marble building. It seems very calm around me—it is very loving and peaceful. Before me there are three beings all dressed in various colored robes. They each possess a certain sense of knowing, as if they know who Josh is and who he has always been. I can only describe them as teachers. As I look into their eyes, I am immediately aware of the life Josh has just lived and who he is as a soul. I hear Josh say: *I realize that I have had many lifetimes in which I was reckless and out of control. I did not respect life. I did not want to participate in life. I always took advantage of people, especially those closest to me. It was the way I got out of doing things and being responsible for my actions. I could always blame someone else if something went wrong. I have felt angry and unwanted in many lives and always found a way to escape.* I am being shown several lifetimes—one in Italy, one in Africa, and his recent life in New Orleans. In each life, Josh tried to overcome this pattern of destroying himself and avoiding responsibility. He says: *I tried to learn to love the person I was.*"

As I came out of trance, I directly faced Josh's sister and said, "In all these lifetimes, I don't see parents, but I do see your energy—once as his twin brother, once as his uncle, and once as his daughter. He is saying: *You have always tried to save me from myself.* The two of you have chosen to come back together to teach each other—your brother to learn responsibility, and you to learn not to take on his troubles. You have to let go of the guilt. That is your pattern."

Josh suddenly began showing me various death scenes from his lifetimes. "This boy is showing me lifetimes of trouble. He bled to death in a cobblestone gutter. He drank himself to death. He died in an opium den in China two centuries ago."

I said to his sister, "You were his lover in that life, and you couldn't save him then either."

Josh's sister began to calm herself.

"In this life, he died of an overdose. Can you see his pattern?"

She nodded her understanding.

"He says that he is working to break this pattern. He wants to thank you for always being there and for taking care of him through these lifetimes. He will be guiding you from heaven."

"Thank you," she said.

As the audience began applauding, Josh sent me a thought of loving appreciation. I knew that his act of charity toward his sister was the step he needed to take to stop feeling unworthy. He was on his way to breaking a soul pattern that had lasted too long. I also knew that his guides were helping to reintegrate his soul energy and make it whole. He left the auditorium within a luminous light.

Soul Groups, Soul Families, and Soul Mates

As Josh's story points out, our souls have experienced many places, times, and situations with the same people. This community of souls that spends numerous lives together is a soul group. A soul group is made up of souls that share the same electromagnetic frequency. As the saying goes: Birds of a feather flock together. A soul group works on a particular theme in order to attain spiritual evolution. A perfect example is the souls gathered on earth today to invent new technology. Many of these souls have been together before—perhaps on different planes of existence or star systems—and have come at this specific time in history to accelerate scientific knowledge. There are also groups of souls today that are making a difference in the earth's environment. Still others are concerned with healing and self-improvement. Because souls are drawn together by their level of spiritual evolution and group purpose, they may participate in one lifetime or several, on the earth plane or in the spiritual realms, to fulfill the particular purpose.

Soul groups are divided into smaller subgroups known as soul families. In a soul family, individuals assist each other more intimately with various lessons. These lessons are based either on previous actions in past-life connections, or on the need to move a soul forward in its spiritual development, or both. A soul family consists of those who interact with us on a daily basis—parents, children, best friends, coworkers, wives, husbands, and even those who oppose us. These souls may come into our lives for a brief period of time or remain with us throughout our entire lives.

As I write this, the rescue of thirty-three miners in Chile is under way. Talk about a spirit family and soul group! Buried a half mile beneath the earth, these men were able to exist in unimaginable conditions for over two months. Others, whom these men had never met, but also members of their soul group, came to their aid and devised a plan to save their lives. Neither wealthy nor prominent, these thirty-three ordinary miners brought the world a powerful message of patience, mutual support, and trust. This event was not an accident, but a spiritual awakening for the planet. There were so many things taking place on so many levels and dimensions that I am sure the long-range positive effects will become clearer over the course of time.

Within our soul family are our soul mates. I believe that we each have many soul mates, not just one, and that these souls have shared special relationships in various incarnations. Soul mates usually feel an overwhelming sense of attraction when they meet. There is a certain sense of being "simpatico," if you will, that is instantly recognizable. Soul mates share a soul memory and have similar values, attractions, likes, and dislikes. Usually they join forces to influence, assist, or teach the individual a significant soul lesson—perhaps one the person has been working on for many lifetimes and in which they have reached a particular turning point. Soul mates may also cause heartache and trouble for us because they have agreed to take on the role of antagonist in order for us to learn self-worth. Remember, too, that soul mates continue to work with you on the spiritual levels once they depart from this lifetime.

Once a soul group finishes the work it sets out to do—and this may take scores of centuries and hundreds of lifetimes—it will disband, and its members can form new groups for a new purpose. Some members may have attained a certain level of enlightenment and may move into the higher spiritual realms to continue learning and growing on those levels.

Ellie's Gift

The following reading shows how a spirit family and soul mates always support one another. In January 2009, I was a guest on the *Beth and Bill* radio show in Phoenix as part of a publicity tour for my latest book, *Unfinished Business*. One of the listeners was a young husband named Frank. He had never heard of me, nor did he believe in psychics or mediums. However, he had recently lost his little girl and, after hearing me speak to loved ones on the other side, he immediately wanted to meet me. Frank showed up at my book signing with his wife, Taunya, and I invited them to attend my spirit circle in Laguna Beach.

The following month, Frank and Taunya walked into the spirit circle and sat down in the front row. They were nervous and tentative, as most people are the first time they take part in something new and different. However, I knew that the event would probably change their lives forever, and it was my task to assist them in any way possible to reach their daughter. Although it turned out to be a remarkable event, the reading was very typical of what happens when spirit families reconnect.

"There is a pretty little girl here around four years old," I said looking at the couple. I see a big L, like EL, or . . ."

Taunya interrupted. "Ellie. Her name is Ellie."

I smiled. "Now she shows me an older woman. This woman brought her into Spirit. Is this her grandmother?"

The couple nodded. "She was very close to my mother, her grandma," said Frank.

"She is showing me the cause of her death now. I see a man. He is drunk. His name is Charles."

I could see Frank's and Taunya's expressions change.

"She died in a car accident," Taunya said. "We were on our way to the store when this car came speeding toward us. The driver was drunk and crashed into our car. Ellie was in the backseat. I lost consciousness."

The room was quiet and still.

"She was not in pain," I continued. "She left her body before the car hit."

Frank and Taunya held hands as they relived this tragic scene once again in their minds.

I continued. "She was about to have a birthday. She was a few days shy of her fourth birthday."

The couple nodded.

"She is showing me a large teddy bear on her bed."

"Yes," Taunya said. "It was a gift from a close family friend."

"Now she is showing me a garden. It's all green—flowers everywhere. There is a butterfly in the garden. She loves the butterfly."

"We have a beautiful garden in Phoenix, and everything seems to grow well, even in the dry climate. Our eight-year-old son, Frankie, planted a flag that has a picture of a butterfly in memory of Ellie."

Some of the people in the room started to cry.

"Now I see Ellie dressed in a prom dress. I don't understand. She's not old enough for a prom, but she is all dressed up in this very fancy dress."

"She was a flower girl in my sister's wedding."

Some oohs and aahs passed through the room.

"I understand. She loved that dress. She felt all grown up," I remarked.

Taunya added, "We have a lot of pictures of her in that dress. It was the dress she was cremated in." Now I could hear a few gasps in the audience.

"I have to tell you, Frank, that I am seeing all these numbers around your head. Lots of numbers."

"I'm a CPA," he responded with a smile.

Everyone laughed.

"Well, that makes sense then," I laughed.

"Your daughter is playing with a puppy. She was very happy when you brought the puppy to her."

"We got her a golden retriever for Christmas," replied Taunya. "We named her Duchess. She and Ellie were very close."

"She is still playing with the dog," I answered, "from the other side."

"Oh, my God," breathed Taunya. "That's why the dog is always bringing her stuff to us—first a sock, then her doll."

"That's your daughter showing you that she's around you. Did she have a necklace? It had a charm."

"Yes, we got that for her."

"I see pennies everywhere. Your daughter is showing me these pennies."

Taunya was startled. "That's my little secret—even Frank doesn't know about it. I save pennies. Oh my gosh. How could you know?"

"Your daughter is showing them to me. She is saying: *Pennies from heaven.*"

Taunya's eyes began to tear up.

"She is showing me a big gift, now. With a really big bow." I said. "This has nothing to do with her death. She is telling me that it has to do with life. *Take it, Mommy,* she says."

Taunya was crying. "After Ellie died, I got pregnant, but I didn't want to have the baby."

"Your daughter is asking you: *Why don't you want the baby, Mommy?* She says the baby was her gift to you. She wanted you to have the baby, and she was telling you to have the baby. It was her gift."

Ellie in her "prom" dress

"We named the baby Maxwell Zane. Zane means 'gift from God,'" Taunya explained.

"You see. Your daughter is helping you from the other side. She is part of your soul family. You are all in the same group."

I listened for anything else that Ellie might have to say. "She is telling me that she helped another girl over. I get the feeling this girl was someone you know. She is saying it was a friend." I looked at Frank. "She means you, Frank."

"Could it be my friend's little girl? My friend lost his girl." Frank was taken aback by this idea.

"That's it. Ellie helped her over into the light."

Taunya and Frank sat there in amazement. I knew that the messages from Ellie had healed them on so many levels.

I spoke to Taunya and Frank before writing their story. They were so grateful for having a second chance at life and for knowing that Ellie was well and thriving in her heavenly home. As is so often the case, it was Ellie who helped them.

Soul Levels

Besides belonging to soul groups and soul families, each soul has a designated purpose based on its level of knowledge, understanding, and awareness. There are many levels of spiritual attainment, but the first four primary levels are the most important for us to understand. These are young souls, mature souls, old souls, and earth angels.

Young souls are at the beginning stages of awareness. They may have had many life experiences or few, lived on this planet or in other dimensions, but their evolution as spiritual beings is, at best, limited. Some of these young, beginner souls may have decided to take a pass through lifetimes and may not have made much headway in learning spiritual values and qualities.

Some may have spent lifetimes with a focus on gaining great positions of power and accumulating large amounts of wealth, having more interest in self-gain and material things than in their own fulfillment and evolution.

Young souls are good at attracting other souls that can propel them to prominence, and have little regard for how their actions affect others. They look at life as a win-or-lose proposition—with winning, of course, being everything. They do not see the big picture, because they live in their own narrow-minded universe seeking only the pleasures of life.

Young souls are ruled by the ego mind, the basis of which is fear. These souls tend to surround themselves with like-minded individuals to form a kind of mutual admiration society. To me, these souls live unconsciously, only looking out for their own needs and wants and ignoring questions of ethics or motives. Many bigoted religious zealots and self-righteous politicians with little tolerance and compassion for anyone with different ideas belong to this group. A majority of young souls inhabit the earth today, at different levels of this beginning stage of spiritual development. Eventually, they will learn their lessons and advance toward maturity.

Mature souls are quite different from young souls, because they are much more conscious of themselves as spiritual beings. They are much more emotionally involved with life, people, and situations. They have well-rounded values and attributes; they tend to be selfless and charitable in their needs and wants. Material possessions do not rule their lives. These souls have genuine consideration for life, whether human, animal, or vegetable. Unlike young souls, mature souls often see life from other points of view. They often question the meaning of life and their purpose for living. They are motivated by usefulness and merit, not profit and loss. Because they are emotionally more open, they experience more emotionally based lessons.

Mature souls handle their responsibilities and think about how their actions impact others' lives. There seems to be much more creativity at this level of awareness; mature souls are well equipped to express their emotionality in artistic and imaginative ways for the entire world to enjoy. Mature souls are the ones that push younger souls to question their motives and beliefs. Their job is to help beginners learn to control their egos, to express sincerity, and to give love and support to others.

Old souls are the most advanced of souls. We have all heard someone refer to another, especially a child, as an old soul. I can say that, based on my observation, children who die young are usually old souls. I really don't think that many of us have a clear idea of what an old soul is, but this is what I know. An old soul is a mature being (age has nothing to do with soul maturity) who has mastered the fundamental issues of life. These souls are utterly patient. They can flow with whatever life brings their way. They are immensely kind and compassionate and fully empathize with others' difficulties.

Old souls are a rare breed on this earth, because they live to enhance human values. Usually, they are not rich or prominent. Most old souls are teachers of life, healers, or light workers. Their aim is to make our world a better place. Some old souls live in remote tribes, healing the earth's electromagnetic grids; others are active in organizations that save starving and abused children; others are in selfless service to the destitute and sick, like Mother Teresa. Old souls know that their mission in life is to serve and to bring their understanding of the world to everyone. Because of their level of awareness, they are much more in step with the rhythm of all life. Old souls usually have many guides in the spirit realm that direct and inspire their work on earth. They maintain a level of personal integrity for which we all strive. Although more advanced, old souls still have something to learn on the physical plane, otherwise they would not incarnate at all. It is rare that a master guide from the spiritual realm returns to earth to enlighten the masses, but it has been done.

Earth angels are radiant souls. I have found that many children who come back to the earth and live for only a short period of time are not only old souls, but also earth angels, here to spread their light to others. These children are well beyond their years on many levels of intelligence, creativity, and personal interaction. They have a natural inclination to draw people to them because of their light. Ellie was such a being—a perfect example of an angel walking upon the earth.

Many earth angels have spent most of their time in higher spiritual realms, occasionally coming to earth to assist someone in their soul group. Although they are part of the human experience, they often feel an overwhelming sense that they don't belong here.

Earth angels have the characteristics of an old soul, along with an intense sense of clarity and a compassionate way of handling others. I can always single out earth angels by looking into their eyes. They have this deep hypnotic gaze from spending lifetimes as extraterrestrials or star people, or as members of more advanced civilizations.

Flight Home

I am not a good flyer. It wasn't so bad when I had just started my career, but now, after having flown around the world many times, and perhaps because of my sensitive nature, I have become extremely uncomfortable when stuck in the metal tube of an airplane for any length of time. Just recently, I was returning home after a teaching weekend at the Omega Institute in New York. My friend Lorna and her husband, Paul, were driving me to Newark Airport to catch a five o'clock flight. I knew that we were running late and expressed my concern. Lorna had more confidence than I did. She said, "There's a lot of traffic, but I'm sure we'll make it." I truly thought I would miss my flight, and I was trying to figure out what to do if I did. Just then, Lorna said, "We'll just have to ask our angels to clear the way!" I took her advice and silently sent out a thought: *Please friends, send me an angel to clear the way, as I am very nervous.*

Lorna and Paul dropped me off, and I scurried around the terminal trying to find the right place to check in. I had not been in Newark Airport for many years, and my anxiety got the better of me. When I looked at my watch, I noticed that I had forty minutes to catch my flight, and I began to freak out. When I reached the counter, I asked the representative, "Will I make the plane?" Seeming less interested in me than she was in chatting with her coworkers, she turned to me and said, "You'll make it." She took my bag and threw it on the conveyor belt. I had a hunch that my bag and I would not reach our destination at the same time. I rushed to the security line, and stared in amazement. It snaked around row upon row. Now, I was frantic. I knew I would never get through the line and would miss my plane for sure.

Suddenly, a young man in a baseball cap standing in front of me turned around and asked, "Are you going to Orange County?"

At that moment, I was shaken out of my worry and responded, "Yes."

"Me, too," he answered. "Don't worry, we'll make the flight. I take it every week. You'll be fine, I promise you."

I looked at his aura and saw an enormous gold ball of light encircling him. I kept on thinking that this must be the angel I had asked for. Suddenly, the line seemed to move a lot faster and, as we advanced toward the checkpoint, we discussed everything from travel to cooking.

As we walked away from the security area toward our gate, he asked, "What do you do?"

I answered, "I'm an author." I never tell people that I'm a medium because, inevitably, the next question is, Is there someone around me?

"What's your name?" I asked.

"Phil," he replied.

"What do you do?"

"I'm a pharmaceutical rep." He then told me the company he worked for.

I thought to myself that that made sense. He sells medication to help people heal.

"What kind of books do you write?" he asked.

I quickly gave my usual response. "Spirituality—books about self-empowerment." He smiled and gave an unexpected response. "Thanks for doing that. The world needs more of that information today."

On the way to the gate, I made a stop at the restroom. "See you on the plane."

"Okeydokey," Phil answered.

Ten minutes later, I arrived at my seat. Guess who was sitting next to me? Phil and I continued to talk all the way to the West Coast.

Are there any earth angels in your life? I'm sure that, if you ask, they will appear.

So knowing that we are souls, and that children who die are old souls, what are we to learn from their deaths? I will discuss the reasons for life and death in the next chapter on soul lessons.

5

Soul Lessons

Souls are not drawn together in physical
life unless there is a strong spiritual
attraction. . . . the attraction of karma. . . .

—WISDOM FROM WHITE EAGLE

W HY WOULD A LOVING GOD be so cruel as to take my child from me? Why do some innocent children have to die before their lives have even begun? Why aren't children spared from violent deaths or tragic accidents? These are some of the questions I am asked at my events and book signings. People think that there must be an easy answer to such questions. The truth is that the answer is simple—and unfortunately, that is why understanding it is even more complex.

These tragedies happen because they are lessons for individual souls, their soul families, and their soul group. In the school of earth, we accumulate lessons based on the way we chose to live in former lifetimes. These become our karmic or soul lessons. The term *karma* comes from ancient Sanskrit and means "action." Karma is a universal law of cause and effect. It is neither good nor bad; it is a choice. A soul chooses to act or react in certain ways through its thoughts, actions, and deeds. In addition to ancient Eastern philosophies, there are various well-documented studies, like Michael Newton's *Journey of Souls* and Andy Tomlinson's *Exploring the Eternal Soul,* that explore the idea of karma and soul lessons. H. P. Blavatsky, founder of the Theosophical Society in 1875, can be called the mother of the modern metaphysical movement. She claimed karma was the ultimate law of the universe, the source, origin, and fount of all other laws that exist throughout Nature. "Karma is the unerring law which adjusts effect to cause, on the physical, mental and spiritual planes of being," she explained. "Karma is that unseen and unknown law which adjusts wisely, intelligently and equitably each effect to its cause, tracing the latter back to its producer." Nowadays, we refer to karma in clichés like "what goes around, comes around." It is karmic law that keeps the universe in balance, governing every person, animal, group, city, nation, and planet.

When a soul reincarnates to earth, it carries all of its past experiences within its soul memory. Whatever a soul created in the past will be revisited in some way. Understanding our behavior and how we affect others is the key to understanding karma.

Free Will vs. Karmic Obligations

If we are here to learn from our past lives, how does free will influence karmic payback? Actually, free will and karma are dependent on, yet in opposition to, each other. One cannot exist without the other. Free will decides our response to particular situations in life. For example, a soul may have had lifetimes of reacting to confrontation with violence. In this life-time, the same soul may set up confrontational circumstances so that it can choose peaceful negotiation rather than violence. Hopefully, by this time, the soul has "learned its lesson" and the soul memory activates a need for change. Instead of acting violently, the soul can make the decision to be understanding; but it is free to choose to be violent again.

Free will means we can always change our minds. Since free will is a part of every decision, young and immature souls can find certain situations especially challenging.

Here is an example. Imagine that you are floating down a river on a raft. Your destination is the river's end, and the ride is your karma. Along the way, you decide to rest on the river-bank for a while. Here, you meet some people. You make the choice to stay and enjoy their company. That is your free will. After a period of time, you get back on the raft and continue the ride because your destination awaits you. The decision to stop was not a part of your original plan, but you did it, and it turned out to be a good choice because you had an enjoyable time.

Here's a more complicated example that shows how most of us are not aware of the cause and effect (karma) involved in events. A man is running late for a business meeting; he has been warned many times not to be late. In his effort to be on time, and because his mind is anxious about the consequences of being late yet again, he runs a red light, plows into a school bus, and kills several children. Had he been more aware of his soul pattern of irresponsibility—running late—he might have started his trip earlier and avoided a collision. We could argue that he caused the death of those children. On the other hand, we could look at it from a different point of view. Perhaps a soul pact existed between the advanced souls of the dead children and the man who collided with the bus. Perhaps, on a spiritual level, they agreed to assist him to change his pattern. I know this is difficult to understand with our human minds. Let's just consider the possibility that, because of the accident, this man realizes the tragic results of his irresponsible behavior and decides to turn his life around. He leaves his job and volunteers to help orphaned children. Once again, he has free will. He can transform his life, or he can retreat into his old pattern of irresponsibility and create more karma to be resolved.

During a lifetime in this school called earth, our reactions to certain experiences impact us sooner or later. Perhaps we have to go through a difficult situation to assist someone else suffering the same thing. Perhaps we have to learn to speak up for ourselves. Or perhaps we have to find a purpose to our lives. I see this time and time again with the death of a child. Parents move into new directions, learn their soul lessons, and grow from the experience. As devastating as these tragedies are, there is a reason for these deaths, as you will learn from the following story.

My Son Saved My Life

Most children touch the earth as angels for a brief period and, in that time, they assist us with our soul lessons. The following reading was a very emotional one, as was the whole night. Several years ago, I was part of a presentation entitled *The Three Mediums* at the El Rey Theater in Los Angeles, sharing the stage with two amazing mediums, Concetta Bertoldi and Rebecca Rosen. Can you imagine three mediums on one stage? To say the least, the night was riveting.

After the break, it was my turn to step on stage. The energy running through the room was powerful. As usual, I rubbed my hands together to feel the force of Spirit. I went through the room calling out to people about their loved ones. One spirit in particular was very insistent.

"Okay," I said looking up. "I'll get to you."

I turned my face to the audience and exclaimed, "There is a spirit here who is very bright and full of love. Has anyone lost a son?"

A few hands went up, but the spirit directed me to a dark-haired petite woman toward the back. A runner handed her a microphone.

"I did," she said.

"This spirit passed very recently. He is very excited to be here. You need to know that this spirit has lived many, many lives and is very evolved spiritually."

Then I turned my head to listen to the young man as he quickly fired off messages.

"Do you have his wallet, please? Because he is telling me you have it."

The woman began shaking and crying at the same time. She looked at the man next to her. Then she turned back to me and nodded. She began rummaging through her purse and finally pulled out the wallet. "This is it."

I addressed the man sitting next to the woman.

"Are you the father?"

He stood up and said, "Yes."

"Your son died very quickly," I said. "His soul left his body very fast. He is saying it was his time to go. Do you understand?"

The petite woman began to cry.

I closed my eyes and listened for the next message.

"Your son's name is Ernest or Ernie?" I asked, looking at the father. "Ernie says thanks for the special wreath. You picked out the flowers. He is showing me a wreath in the shape of a heart. He liked that you put his picture in the middle of the heart."

Ernie's dad was filled with emotion.

The woman looked at her husband and asked, "Is this true?"

The father cried and nodded.

I opened my arms very wide and said, "He wants you to have the heart. You were a great dad—the best. He thanks you for that."

"He says he loves you both very much. He wants you to know that. He says he picked you especially as his parents and wants you to know that you will always be together."

Then I turned to the mother and remarked, "He is showing me a blue ribbon with #1 Mom on it. He wants you to know that you were a great mother. He loves you. *I have the best parents,* he is saying. *You are both very special.*"

Both parents were speechless.

"Now he is showing me a small beach. It has a pier or a bridge. He was there with you. He was trying to help you."

The woman began to sob.

"He has a great big smile. Did he play football? Because he is showing me a football jersey."

"Yes, he did."

"He is moving as if he were skating." I tried to sway side to side as the spirit was showing me.

"He loved to skateboard."

"I want you to know that your son is a very evolved spirit. Do you understand?"

"Yes."

Suddenly, Ernie sent me another thought.

"Does the name Lucy or Lucille mean anything to you?"

I could see the surprise on his parents' faces, as if lightning had struck from out of the blue. A few rows behind the couple, there was a man who began to sob uncontrollably. The woman turned her head to look at him and said, "My Ernie is really here!"

The man a few rows back nodded to her, but couldn't speak because he was crying so hard.

"Lucy is our dog. I had her euthanized the morning my son died."

A gasp rose from the audience.

"He is telling me that Lucy was waiting for him." Then I said, "He wants you to be happy." At that point, I felt the reading was over, and I turned to walk away, but the young man urged me to go back.

"He does not want to leave you. He is very insistent. How did he pass?"

Just before the woman spoke, the spirit showed me an image. "He is showing me a gun, but this has nothing to do with his passing. Do you understand? He is very concerned about you. The gun is in a closet."

"We own guns," said the mother. "I thought of shooting myself with it."

Another gasp emerged from the audience.

I looked at the woman and could feel her pain and sorrow. I shook my head. "Please, don't," I said. "Your son has come here tonight to tell you not to. Your son is trying to help you. He wants you to live. It is not your time. You both have work to do on the earth."

As I looked at this woman, I could see her standing on a bridge in deep despair.

"You think about killing yourself a lot."

"Yes. I understand. Tell my son I won't think about killing myself ever again."

I knew that young Ernie was there not only to help his parents, but to help all the parents who felt so utterly hopeless and alone.

When Ernie was satisfied that his mother was okay and would no longer try to kill herself, he left in a vapor of light.

I asked the couple to stay afterward so that we could chat. When the event was over, I stood on the balcony of the beautifully ornate theater and met Martha and Ernesto, Ernie's parents, and their friend James, the man who had been sitting a few rows behind them. Martha told me about Ernie's death in a terrible car crash on his way home from work. She and her husband owned some gift shops on the *Queen Mary,* and her son ran the ship's boutique. She spoke about the heartbreak of putting their dog Lucy to sleep the very same day her son had died.

Martha also told me how Ernie had been in two previous accidents. "He was supposed to go in the first one," I said.

"Why did he stay?" Martha asked.

"He still had things to do."

She then expressed how she hadn't wanted to live, but reassured me that the gift of their son's message would help both of them.

"You're never alone," I told them.

Recently, I received a follow-up e-mail from Martha.

Dear James,

I wish I had the words to describe what I feel for you. I don't know you well, but I think of you often and send you good thoughts and our love. You saved my life in so many ways. The morning after your reading, I could feel myself awaken and waited for the feeling of hopelessness and utter despair to get ahold of me, but it did not come. I opened my eyes, thought of Ernie, and smiled. I felt my heart fill with hope. I told him that I loved him and thanked him for being there. You and Ernie saved my life, James. After that night I went back to work every day. I wanted to be involved again. I wanted to be in his store surrounded by the people he loved and who loved him. I knew that he was watching me, and I needed him to be proud of me again. I have hope now. I know that we are not alone and that, when my time comes, I will see him again. I know this with total certainty. He will run to meet me and give me an Ernie hug and I will be whole again. His father carries me and I carry him. Our strength comes from having shared our lives with Ernie. Thank you, James. Wherever you are, whatever you do, I will always send you our love and good thoughts.

Martha

This family had been together through many lifetimes. Although Ernie's work was done on earth, it was not yet finished in Spirit. He had to keep his mother from making a terrible mistake. In so doing, he fulfilled a very important karmic obligation to save his mother's life. Perhaps, in another life, his mother had saved him from making a similar error in judgment. When a child dies, no matter its age, the death is undoubtedly a lesson for the parent(s).

Before incarnating on the earth sphere, souls choose the lessons and karmic obligations they need to fulfill with the aid of their spirit families and the Council of Elders. These lessons are mostly unresolved issues left over from previous lifetimes, as I had surmised in the reading above. When in Spirit, a soul

makes a conscious commitment to learn, but when it reincarnates, this memory is clouded over by human emotions—
or as I say, human amnesia. Questions always arise as well
about children born with certain mental conditions or physical
handicaps. I can only relate what the spirit world has shared
with me. No doubt there is a spiritual drama being played out,
so I ask that you not judge any situation. All circumstances
are chosen to help us learn the many aspects of love. Over the
years, I have been given spiritual insights into these lessons
and would like to share what I know.

Miscarriage, Abortion, and Infant Fatality

Miscarriages are soul contracts between mother and child.
An unborn soul may be testing the mother's commitment, or
testing itself as to whether or not it wants to live in a physical body. The soul may come into the mother, realize it is not
ready, and leave. And it may do this several times. The same
soul may be helping the mother learn her lessons, which may
be about control (I need to get pregnant now) or self-doubt (I
want to get pregnant, but I really want to get that promotion).
Other lessons may be about health or finances. The unborn
soul may be giving her a chance to put her house in order before deciding to attach itself to the womb permanently. I have
brought through many spirits that have said that it just wasn't
the right time for either them or the mother.

From a spiritual perspective, abortions are lessons for the
mother to learn self-love and self-worth. In the case of abortion, the soul always knows that the fetus will be aborted
and does not attach itself to the physical body of the unborn.
Therefore, no one is murdered in an abortion. Here again, both

souls have agreed that they will go through this experience for growth. This matter can also be about one soul paying back a karmic debt to the other. Perhaps in a prior lifetime, the soul of the unborn was a mother who gave away her child and so must feel the effects of abandonment and/or betrayal.

Several mothers have written to me expressing their feelings in making such a decision. One mother had five children, no money, no husband, and was in so much misery and pain about making her decision to abort that she thought of ending her own life. Her guilt was overwhelming. Punishing this mother would be a tragedy for her other children. Another mother wrote about how she was visited by the soul of the unborn the night before the abortion. She shared that the soul had found another mother and that it acknowledged her decision and loved her. It is not for us to judge these soul lessons.

Those who die from sudden infant death syndrome and other infant diseases are usually advanced souls who need only the birth experience to fulfill their purpose and help parents with soul growth. Again, this agreement was made prior to the incarnation. Another possibility may be that the soul made a hasty decision to reincarnate and, after a short period of existence, decided it was not ready to fulfill its obligations. On occasion, souls have communicated that they decided to learn their lessons with a different group of souls than their current family. In all cases, the death of the child forces parents to appreciate life and keep their focus on love.

Childhood Illness and Accidents

Have you ever noticed that a child who is sick is more concerned about its parents' welfare than its own? When a child dies from disease, the situation is always about teaching others. Perhaps the lessons have to do with compassion, unselfish giving, or unconditional love. There is also the possibility that a soul goes through an illness so that future generations will not have to. This was obviously the case during the polio epidemic of the early 1950s. I remember seeing newsreels about children standing in long lines to get their precious polio vaccine. It's unfortunate, and yet expected, that some souls will pay the price of life so that millions can be saved.

What appears to us as an arbitrary accident is already known in the spiritual realm. In other words, accidents are not accidents; they are predetermined. This applies to car and bus accidents, airplane and train crashes, drownings, falls, fires, and any other so-called mishaps. Natural disasters like tsunamis, tornadoes, and earthquakes are usually preplanned by many soul groups in order to teach love and compassion to the rest of us. It is no wonder that, when a disaster hits a city or a country, everyone from around the world pitches in to help the victims and their families. This is a lesson of soul expansion and transformation, especially for those left behind. Accidents and disasters often trigger new laws or new ways of protecting the general population or those less fortunate. In many cases, these "accidental" deaths cause parents and others to question their spiritual beliefs. When speaking to the spirits of children who died in accidents, I have learned that the major lesson for parents is to let go of their guilt and forgive themselves.

That was the case with Vanessa's mother, who was so full of self-blame that her daughter had a difficult time getting through to her. At an event in British Columbia, before the very last reading of the evening, a young, beautiful female spirit appeared before me.

"There is a seventeen-year-old girl with long fair hair. Her mother is in the audience, and she has a lock of the girl's hair in her purse."

Now, what happened next happens all too often. The mother I was addressing was too afraid to stand up, so I went on.

"She is showing me a doll. Does this mean anything?"

A woman in the back of the room raised her hand.

"Please stand up, so we can get a microphone to you."

The woman stood up.

"Is this your daughter?" I asked.

"No, she's my niece."

"Is she seventeen years old?"

"No. My niece was eighteen."

I shook my head, because I knew this was not the right person. The spirit was telling me: *It's not her.*

"Okay. She is showing me a lock of hair. Do you have a lock of her hair with you?"

"I have a lock of her hair, but I didn't bring it. It's at home. I asked my sister for it."

"I see a hospital. She wasn't happy there."

I went on for a few more minutes, trying to establish a connection between the spirit and the woman in front of me.

I began to tap my left wrist. "Was she on an IV? Something on her wrist?"

The woman shook her head no.

"She is showing me a long, white dress from around the time she passed. She looks very beautiful."

Still no response from the woman.

I began waving my hands in front of me. "This girl is showing me lots of pictures—lots and lots of pictures."

Feeling frustrated, the final impression I received was of flowers. "She loves all the flowers that you planted."

I became more convinced that the person standing in the audience was not the right person, but, since the real mother didn't stand, I had to end the reading. "She is telling me that her mother is in a lot of pain. Could you ask your sister to contact me on my website, please?"

The woman nodded and sat down.

All the while, the real mother of this girl was in the audience. Right after that demonstration, she contacted my website. The following is an excerpt from her letter.

Dear James,

In June 1999, our lives changed forever. That was the day our seventeen-year-old daughter, Vanessa, died as a result of a car accident. A few weeks following her death, someone who understood the pain and sorrow we were going through mailed us a copy of *Talking to Heaven*. It started my husband and me on a journey that has had an amazing result. We discovered the world of mediums and read many different books by several authors. We even visited one in our city for a personal reading, but that experience was so devastatingly painful that it left me a virtual skeptic. We have both believed over the years that Vanessa's spirit was nearby. My husband, Curtis, had heard from her many times, but she was very silent to me. Although they gave us a sense of pleasure, I wondered if we found these signs because we had the need for them.

In 2008, after watching *The Bucket List*, like thousands of others I made up my wish list. I wanted to experience a true, world-renowned medium and preferred you. Your books were the ones that seemed to give me the most comfort. Over the next couple of years, I checked your website to see if you were going to be in Vancouver

so we could go to the show. In the meantime, my friend
Laurie invited me to go with her to a psychic. This visit
was also painful. All I wanted to hear was a message
from Vanessa but, because of my skepticism, I could not.
I left the reading in tears after hearing the psychic tell
me that I was in too much pain to hear from Vanessa.
Then the coincidences started to happen. They ended
one morning when I turned on the TV and heard the
announcer mention that you were coming to Vancouver.

While I waited for the night to come, I thought long
and hard about what I would take with me. My decision
was a lock of Vanessa's beautiful, long blond hair. At the
show, you started to talk about how the messages were
for everyone. You began the last reading of the night
by describing a young girl with long fair hair and asked
if her mother was in the audience. I froze. I couldn't
believe what I had heard. I had forgotten her lock of hair,
leaving it at home. No one put up his or her hand, so you
mentioned a doll. I thought about how that could relate
to Vanessa—she had dozen of dolls—and then another
lady put up her hand. I wanted to scream, but the books
on mediums all say not to give too much away.

As we went to the car, I said to Curtis, "That was
Vanessa." He asked me why I didn't put up my hand.
I was so upset. It was my fault. I had failed yet again
as a mother, and I had taken the opportunity away
from Curtis to hear from her. I was so afraid to be
disappointed and hurt as before. I was afraid that I would
say too much, because I wanted it so much, and that I
would make anything you said fit. All the way home,
I beat myself up with the same "what if" feelings of
inadequacy that I had about the car accident. I couldn't

sleep that night. I was reliving how I had asked for an
opportunity to talk to Vanessa and, when it happened,
I froze.

I analyzed every word you said—a seventeen-year-
old girl with long fair hair, the lock of hair, the doll
(it hit me that I had made dolls for Vanessa and her
sister and embroidered on the hem, "Wherever you go,
whatever you do, be happy, and remember that I love
you.") Then you mentioned the hospital. Yes, she was
in a hospital after the accident, and they could not save
her. You tapped your wrist—I bought her a watch for her
birthday. The long white dress—her graduation dress was
a very pale yellow. She wore it three weeks prior to the
accident and looked so beautiful in it. The pictures—I
know everyone has lots of pictures, so I dismissed that
comment. But Curtis had bought a large Tupperware
container and filled it with twenty albums. The day of
the event, I had put pictures all over the desk, floor, and
cabinets—lots and lots of pictures. The last thing you
mentioned was flowers—we had just been talking about
the flowers that we planted in the front of our house at
dinner prior to the show.

There were too many coincidences. I finally got up
and went to the computer, remembering that you had
asked the mother to contact you via your website. I sent
an e-mail. That night, I went to bed doubting myself
and feeling like a failure again. At 3:00 A.M., I woke up.
(Vanessa's favorite number was three). I lay there talking
to Vanessa. When Curtis woke up, we talked. Everything
fell into place. It was okay that I didn't put my hand up.
It was a lesson I had to learn. I could believe in the power
of spirits to speak through mediums. She knew that I

was afraid to be hurt again, and that I really wanted to believe, so she kept talking to you, giving you all the clues so I could know it was Vanessa. Suddenly, it was crystal clear. You are the medium, but the messages only make sense if it is the right connection. To make sure I got it, the light outside in our backyard went on for a few seconds, then went out. I really had seen the light. Vanessa was okay. I really did understand her messages after all. I can stop feeling like a failure and start to heal. I am open to feel her love. Thank you for helping.

    Cheryl

When fearful emotions take control of us, as they had Cheryl, it is impossible to be open to or aware of Spirit. Vanessa had given her mother many clues, but Cheryl had to let go of her fear and pain, and the sway of other people's opinions.

Cheryl and Vanessa will have many opportunities to reunite as a soul family, and even more opportunities to learn from one another. In the next chapter, we will see how a soul makes a decision to be with its spirit family and decides the lessons it wants to learn. Then we'll see how all this takes place before we come back to earth.

Suicide

Suicide is the one act that I'm not sure is planned on the other side. Every situation is different. When a suicide's soul passes over and realizes the devastation and pain it has caused its family and friends, the soul feels not only their depth of pain, but regret. Suicides realize that their problems did not disappear, and that they still have to come to terms with certain feelings. Through the years, I have learned that the intention behind suicide is of the utmost importance. For instance, a person who commits suicide because someone bullied her or him is handled differently from a person with a mental illness. In the first instance, the person used free will, decided not to go through with the soul lesson, and opted out before the time was up. A person with a mental disorder may have tried to overcome some karmic lesson, but the soul was too damaged to hang on. Also, souls that rush back into new lives before they have perfected the soul lessons from previous lives often feel that they do not fit in and want to leave. This was exactly what happened to my cousin Patricia—who, by the way, was the person who introduced me to metaphysics when I was a young boy.

The most important thing to remember in a suicide is that a soul wants to learn and grow, and if the soul has chosen to end its journey (cut school) early, it will, of course, have to come back and repeat its classes. Remember that the soul can never be harmed or hurt; its lessons are those of self-love, love for others, patience, and faith. The best thing we on earth can do for those who commit suicide is to forgive them and love them unconditionally. Our love and forgiveness make it easier for them to love and forgive themselves on the spirit side of life.

Murder

Of course, each murder situation is unique. Murder can be a karmic lesson or payback for a previous karmic debt. It may involve someone on a low level of spiritual evolution, or a young soul repeating a destructive soul pattern. The number one lesson in this circumstance is forgiveness. I believe we must forgive and assist these souls to realize the harmful repercussions of their actions. If we understand that we are spirits playing out physical experiences in order to evolve, it helps to appreciate the variety of situations that occur.

In England, at an event that was part of a publicity tour of television appearances and book signings, I gave a reading that brought tears to everyone in the house. At the end of the question-and-answer part of the event, spirits began lining up, and some of them were quite eager to get my attention.

"I have two boys standing behind my right side. They are very anxious to get someone's attention here. They must be around eight and ten years old. They are telling me it's very important. They both have light blond hair and blue eyes. Does this make sense to anyone here?"

I waited for someone to raise a hand. While I waited, I asked the two boys for more information.

"Oh, I see." I looked out at the audience and said, "Now, there is another young boy here, about six or seven. So there are three boys standing here."

Suddenly, there was an outcry from the middle of the auditorium. I looked toward that section of the room and saw one of the runners handing a microphone to a woman standing in the middle of a row.

"Do you recognize these boys?" I asked the woman.

"My brother lost his three sons at about that age."

"They are showing me a car. Now they are riding in the car. This is the scene of their death."

"Yes. Those are my brother's boys."

"What is your name, please?"

"Margaret. I am their aunt."

"Margaret, these boys are showing me the car in the water now. They are in the car in the water and they cannot get out. They drown in the water."

"Yes, that is how they died," she said with a numbness in her voice.

"One of them, the older boy, is telling me to say they are okay. *We are okay,* he keeps repeating. *Don't cry anymore. Tell Dad not to cry anymore.*"

Margaret broke down and started to cry. "Oh, my God. Those poor boys."

"I'm getting Henry or Herman, something with a Hen."

"Hayden. The oldest boy was Hayden."

"He is saying: *Don't blame Mum. She was not to blame. We love her.*"

This remark set the woman off once more. She put her hands to her face. Another younger woman stood up next to her.

"I'm Lindsey, her daughter."

"Thank you," I replied. "These boys are very anxious about their dad. They want him to know about them. They are showing me a computer. They have been trying to get through on the computer to him.

At this point, Lindsey also put her hand to her mouth. "My uncle sells software. He always has a computer with him."

"Well, tell him that they are trying to tell him they are okay."

"What about their mother?" Lindsey asked.

I sent my thoughts to the three young boys and asked if they could tell me more. At that point, they showed me something I never expected to see. Their mother is putting them in the car and then driving to what looks like a dock. She sits there for a while talking to them, and then she drives the car into the water. The car goes down very quickly. She gets out, but the boys remain in the car.

I looked over at Margaret and Lindsey. "I see their death more clearly," I said to them. "Their mother drowned them, didn't she?"

The whole audience moaned in horror.

"Yes," said the young woman. "That vile woman drowned her three young sons."

The pain this family had been going through was very clear to me. I could sense the enormous anger and hate aimed at the mother.

"There was something more at play here. This woman had some mental and emotional issues. The boys want you to forgive her. They love their mother. They were here to help her and they all left together. She did nothing wrong in their eyes."

"She murdered her children!" cried Margaret.

"Yes, she did and she will be punished for that in this life. However, you came here to hear from Spirit, and these boys forgive their mother. They were part of a bigger plan. Their mother needed their help and they were willing to help her. They want their dad to forgive her, too."

I knew that this was very difficult to comprehend.

Margaret spoke. "He has been hounded by the tabloids for months, and he hasn't been able to sleep since all of this happened."

"Please, let him know that his boys are okay. Hayden is telling me that they have been playing with their father's computer. They want him to know that they are with him and will always be with him. Will you tell him that, please?"

Margaret shook her head. "It will be difficult. He is totally shattered."

My heart went out to this woman and her brother. Then I was shown something else.

"The littlest boy is smiling and showing me a book with a moon and stars on the cover."

"*Goodnight Moon*," Margaret said. "It was Perry's favorite."

"Tell his dad to read him the book at night. He will be listening."

"Oh, God. I'm not sure if I can."

"Please try," I said. "It will help them both."

"All right."

"They are smiling now and waving good-bye."

Then I said to the audience: "Pray for this father and this family. Your prayers are always heard and they will help. Those little boys are really God's angels."

At this point, there was not a dry eye in the house.

This was the first time I had ever done a reading about this type of tragic event, so a few days later I did a little sleuthing on the Internet. I was amazed at all the incidents of mothers killing their children that have occurred—and not just in a few places, but all around the world. I believe these situations are truly karmic. Many of the mothers in the cases that I read had committed suicide or were committed to mental wards. The soul lessons are very individualistic. In this particular reading, it was apparent that the boys very much wanted their father to forgive their mother. That was the message they came to impart. I also must tell you that, if someone does not forgive and holds on to pain, anger, hate, guilt, or whatever, the negative energy will bleed into other parts of that person's life and onto all those who share it.

Reunion

Many parents say that the most important thing they have learned from their deceased children is that, one day, they will be reunited; of this, they have no doubt. In the next chapter, we will explore the factors involved in returning to earth and a soul's opportunities to learn and grow.

To end this chapter, I will share a beautiful poem written by acclaimed British medium Doris Stokes, who passed in 1987. "Many years ago," she tells us, "whilst I was grieving over the loss of my baby, the spirit world gave me a poem, which has been a great comfort to me all these years. I hope this poem will bring comfort to parents who have lost children."

MY BABY

In a baby castle just beyond my eye
My baby plays with angel toys that money cannot buy.
Who am I to wish him back,
into this world of strife?
No, play on my baby,
you have eternal life.
At night when all is silent
And sleep forsakes my eyes,
I'll hear his tiny footsteps come running to my side.
His little hands caress me,
so tenderly and sweet,
I'll breathe a prayer,
close my eyes and embrace him in my sleep.
Now I have a treasure that I rate above all others,
I have known true glory—I am still his mother.

6

The Soul Returns

And the day came when the risk to remain
tight in a bud was more painful than
the risk it took to blossom.

—ANAÏS NIN

A S THE SOUL PASSES through the spirit world, it realizes
that it has entered a sphere of creative energy, universal thought, compassion, joy, and quiet contemplation. It is a very productive place that is designed to help the
soul study, gain knowledge, and mature. Here, souls reunite
with their spirit families and soul groups to work on their soul
lessons and plan their next earthly missions. In this inter-life,
or between lives in the earthly realm, souls can progress to
higher forms of consciousness. As I said in chapter 3, souls go
to schools where they can specialize in various interests that
will assist in future incarnations. Souls may want to expand
their creative gifts; for instance, if they have a talent for singing or dancing, they may work to perfect these abilities.

Eventually, a soul will feel a pull to life outside the spiritual
world so that it can broaden its horizons even further. When a

soul chooses to reincarnate, it can do so not only on earth, but also on other planets, star systems, and galaxies. A soul can incarnate in many forms other than a physical body. It may choose to be a vaporous being, a water form, or even an animal. Life offers a variety of existences and, with each choice, a soul maps out specific lessons that fit the specific environment. If a soul chooses to return to earth, it will ready itself for human lessons.

A soul has a good understanding of the lessons necessary for transformation and always has a choice whether to progress or not. It can stay in the inter-life as long as it wants and can progress spiritually there; however, growth will be much slower. Our physical world works directly with emotions and offers a variety of hardships and challenges not found on any other dimension. Sometimes the choice to return to earth is a difficult one, because, to a spiritual being, earth seems unnatural and lacking in love. It is a world filled with fear, uncertainty, aggression, and naiveté. On the other hand, earth definitely provides many of life's pleasures, which a soul remembers with great sentimentality. Because earth is a marvelous schoolroom where a soul's spiritual ideals are tested, a soul may return to earth many times for the opportunity to perfect its strength and neutralize past karma. By reincarnating to earth, souls progress very rapidly.

Reincarnation has been an enduring belief for thousands of years and is a part of almost every modern culture. It was once a part of Christianity, until it was eradicated in 325 AD by the Roman Emperor Constantine at the Council of Nicaea in an effort to unite various feuding factions of his empire. In order to fully understand the concept of reincarnation, we must let go of the preconceived restraints of linear time and space that limit our three-dimensional world. Time is only relative to a three-dimensional existence; it is a way to measure progress or change. In Spirit, there is no time; there is only now. Past, present, and future are simultaneous, and choices made in our current life affect our past and future lives as well.

Planning Your Next Life

When a soul decides to reincarnate to earth, it meets with two distinct levels of beings. The first is a community of guides that either has been with the soul during many lifetimes or is entirely new. The other group is a Council of Elders or master teachers—the same group it met upon its departure from a physical body and its return to its spiritual home. Both groups assist the soul with its next-life plan by helping it to understand the experiences necessary for growth. Thus, past karma is evaluated on an individual, family, economic, social, and spiritual basis, and is threaded through the soul's make-up. All essential ingredients are planned into the next life in order for the soul to advance up the spiritual ladder.

After considering various factors that pertain to its evolution, a soul and its guides plan the perfect time and place for the next incarnation. They preview several life scenarios and choose the one that fits best. This preview can be observed in several ways, according to inter-life specialist Dr. Michael Newton and past-life regressionist Dr. Ian Stevenson, both of whom have done extensive research in this area. To understand this with our human minds, it would be as if a soul can view a potential life in a theater setting using 3-D, stop-motion action, observing various environments and conditions. Another way a soul can preview a life is in an arena-style setting with multiple screens that project a sampling of lives with an assortment of people and places.

Choosing a new life is based on many factors—the goals a soul wants to achieve, karmic patterns and debts it wants to balance, or the culture and environment it wants to experience. All these factors have a significant influence on a soul's choice. My personal theory about déjà vu experiences is that they may originate with this inter-life preview, coming into a person's awareness the moment he or she "re-lives" the projected experience seen in the life-selection process.

Even with all the help and guidance from soul mates and guides on the other side, sometimes a soul will not take all the steps needed to plan extensively and will rush its return to the earth realm, reincarnating too soon after it has arrived in the spiritual realm. Remember that souls have the free will to do as they please, even if the odds are stacked against them. This is what happened to this young soul who returned to earth before the optimum time.

Lucky 13

The following story was posted to my website by a mother who attended a demonstration in Arizona.

My friend and I arrived early and grabbed the closest available seats in the second row. Within a few minutes, I realized that I was sitting in the thirteenth chair. Tears began to flow, because I knew my daughter was with me. Thirteen was her number. She was born on the thirteenth; she tattooed the number on herself; she named her art gallery Lucky 13. After the break, James answered questions from the audience. He seemed a little irritated and kept glancing over his right shoulder.

"I can only take one more question," he said. "I've got a young girl here, and she is a pain in the ass! She came to me backstage on break, and she wants to speak now."

I immediately got chills and thought, "Oh God, Michele, wait your turn, honey."

James went on to describe Michele in detail, as an artist who loved her hair, had money problems, and committed suicide. My hand went up, but James kept talking. I had no idea if there were any other hands raised, but I understood every detail of what he was saying.

Finally, he looked at me and asked, "What is her name?."

Someone handed me a microphone and I responded, "Michele."

"She is saying Micky.."

"Yes, that is what her friends call her."

"I see her cutting herself in the bathroom. It has black and white tiles."

I nodded my head in acknowledgment. I didn't tell him about all the times throughout the years that she had cut herself, or about the emergency-room visits to get her stitched up.

James grinned. "She has a sweetness about her."

"You just called her a pain in the ass; both are true! My mom always used the word 'sweetness' to describe Michele."

James said, "She had a drug problem. She came back too soon. She wasn't ready. She didn't feel as if she fit in. She had abuse and trust issues."

Again, I nodded in acknowledgment.

"Who's Jean?" James asked.

"My mom."

"She needs to stop worrying."

"I know. Michele and I lived with my parents for the first three years of her life; she was their daughter, too."

"Who is Judy? The one in spirit."

"That's my friend Judy."

"How did she die?"

"The same way," I said.

"Yes. They are together. They are helping each other."

I couldn't even talk. I had pictures of Michele and Judy with me. Judy's sister and I had joked about the two of them finding each other; they had so much in common, and they would have a lot of mischievous fun together.

Then he said, "She is saying: *Tats, tats, tats.*"

"Tattoos," I said. "She was an incredible artist. When she wasn't painting, she designed tattoos and tattooed herself and all of her friends." The skeptic in me was wondering if James was reading my mind: how could he know all of this?

Then he said, "She is showing me a raccoon's tail. Do you understand this?"

Instantly, I got an image in my mind and couldn't help but laugh out loud through my tears. It was Michele's way of kicking my skeptical butt, and making sure there was no doubt that she was there.

"Oh, my God," I said. "It was a sex toy I found in Michele's apartment years ago. She tried to explain it to me, but I didn't understand. I don't know the name, but I know what you are saying."

James laughed. "This girl is kinky."

Everyone laughed.

James took a few minutes and talked to the audience about suicide. I can't remember what he said, because my mind was busy thanking Michele for making me breathe; for making me laugh.

James finished up my reading by telling me what I knew in my heart—that Michele was with me and that she was happier on the other side.

There are many reasons for suicide, but for Michele, it was that she had returned to earth without the proper preparation. That is why she tried to leave the earth so many times, until she finally succeeded. Michele was quickly reunited with her soul group and spirit guides and has learned that she must be fully prepared when the time comes for her next incarnation.

Choosing a Body

Once a life selection is made, a soul must also pick the type of body it will inhabit in its chosen environment. Here again, a soul, with the assistance of its guides, previews a sampling of bodies and chooses race, gender and sexual orientation. A body has to serve a soul's best interest to accomplish the lessons and goals it has planned. For instance, if a soul needs to learn self-worth, it may come back as a gorgeous model. The lesson is to recognize the beauty within.

It can be difficult for a soul to see its true value when all around are judging only outward appearances. This is very much how I felt about Jennifer Love Hewitt, who played Melinda on my show *The Ghost Whisperer*. The tabloids were relentless in making terrible remarks about her body. She had to have a good sense of her inner value in order to deflect such harsh criticism. In truth, she is not her body, but a beautiful soul. That is what we all should recognize. Fortunately, Jennifer was smart enough to realize that beauty is only skin deep. Unfortunately, she is in a business that is stereotypically shallow and sees only what it can sell. I felt the whole publicity attack was a soul lesson that Jennifer had brought with her from another lifetime—something she needed to perfect in this one.

As a soul evaluates its possible bodies, it must also be aware of any potential handicap or health crisis associated with that body and whether it will or will not endure. Valuable information, accumulated and retained from past lifetimes, is imbedded in the soul memory. Finally, a soul decides on personality, opportunities, and any turning points in its upcoming experience. All of this affects the type of body chosen, as you will appreciate from the following reading.

I Have the Perfect Body

Scott and Linda came to one of my demonstrations on a whim. It was the first time they had ever seen a medium, or even a psychic for that matter. They were visiting a cousin, and their cousin purchased tickets to see me, so they decided to tag along. It was a choice that changed their lives; their minds opened, never to be closed again.

I had just finished bringing a message through to a man from his father in spirit. I turned around to take a sip of water, and then turned back toward the audience. Suddenly, I was aware of a red-headed boy rolling his wheelchair straight down the aisle.

"Wow!" I thought. I shared my observation with the audience. "There is a teenage boy here with red hair who was about seventeen when he passed. He is in a wheelchair."

As I spoke, I saw the boy maneuver his wheelchair into the middle of an aisle, all the while sending me his thoughts.

"He says he came to see Linda and Scott."

At that point, the stunned couple on the aisle next to this spirit looked at each other like two deer caught in headlights. They didn't know what to do next.

"Are you Linda and Scott?" I asked.

The shaken couple stood up slowly.

"Yes," the man replied.

"Hi!" Linda declared in a high-pitched voice. She was holding on to her husband for dear life. "This is crazy. Are you sure you're talking to us?" she asked in disbelief.

I looked directly at the couple. "Did you have a teenage boy with red hair who was in a wheelchair when he passed?"

Linda started to sob as Scott held her up and answered the questions, choking back tears. "We did. That was our boy, Clarke."

Then Clarke did something quite amazing—something I had rarely seen in demonstrations. He rose out of the wheelchair, morphed into a wondrous being of light, and stood between his parents as he transmitted thoughts.

"He is such a beautiful spirit," I said. I, too, became very emotional as I tuned in to his energy. "He is quite an evolved being, and I just want to say that I am honored to bring him through for you tonight."

"Oh, thank you. I appreciate it," Scott answered.

The emotional moment was broken when Linda let out an innocent, yet wonderful, insight. "My golly, you are the real deal! I thought it was all a TV show."

The audience and I laughed.

I responded, "Well Linda, your love is real and that is what brought him here tonight."

Clarke proceeded to present a stream of information mixed with spiritual insights.

"He wants to thank you both for sharing this lifetime with him. He is telling me that you took him in when nobody wanted him. He is saying: *I was looked down upon.*"

"Yes, that's right," replied Scott.

"We were not able to have children of our own, but we prayed to God for help. I knew that one day when we least expected it, our child would find us and give us a sign, and we would know him the moment we saw him," said Linda.

Clarke showed me another scene.

"Was he adopted?" I asked. "Because I am seeing a hallway and a waiting room with pictures of children on the walls. Did you go to an adoption agency?"

"Yes, we went to more than twenty of them," answered Linda.

"Why so many?"

Linda looked at me as if I had asked a stupid question.

"We didn't have our sign," she blurted out.

"And then it happened," said Scott. "We got our sign."

At that point, the entire audience was on the edge of their seats. I could see Clarke grinning from ear to ear.

Without missing a beat, Scott said, "He kicked me!"

Linda started laughing.

Scott continued, "We were standing in the hall waiting for the administrator, and this little red-haired kid came zooming down the hall in his wheelchair, ran over my left foot, and gave me a kick in my right ankle."

The audience roared with laughter.

Linda continued the story. "We both were kind of in shock. Then we looked down and saw the face of an angel! We had never seen a child like him before; he was so beautiful. We knew he was ours; he was the one God had sent us."

Linda's words were interrupted by Clarke's thoughts. "Clarke is telling me that he was fully disabled as well."

"Oh, yeah," said Scott. "He had everything wrong with him—muscular dystrophy, mild retardation, Tourette's syndrome—you name it, he had it. He was off the charts!"

I could tell the audience was mesmerized.

Linda had quite a curious look on her face. She stared at me as if I should have known. "That's what made him all the more special, James."

Clarke proceeded to send more information. "He wants to thank you for seeing beyond his disabilities and into his soul. He wants me to tell you and the audience that he picked his physical body. He did this for many reasons, but the most important lesson had to do with teaching other people about compassion. Anyone who ever met him, he tells me, looked past his disability, and only saw his light."

Scott nodded.

Linda said, "That's exactly right. If you were with him for a few minutes, you completely forgot about the wheelchair."

"He is also telling me that you all picked each other out this time around in order to make progress in a spiritual sense, and to show others how they can overcome anything. Not only did you work with him in assisting his soul, you also started a group or did something with a school. Is that right?" I asked.

Linda replied. "Yes, we started a specialized school program for the disabled, which has been recognized by the state. Any teacher with a disabled student in class must go through this course to understand how to treat the child. These children are not victims, but human beings like everyone else. I believe they teach us instead of the other way around."

The audience applauded.

"This lady has done a lot," said Scott. I could feel the love he had for his wife.

Clarke sent me another thought. "Did Clarke play the piano?"

Linda immediately put her hands to her face and murmured, "Oh no."

Scott responded. "Yes. Linda taught him. I remember the day I walked into the house and saw Clarke playing the piano with his feet."

Linda added, "He was so quick to catch on. Music was the only thing that could soothe him."

"He tells me that you used to communicate with him heart to heart. He wants you both to know that you are constantly building other people's self-esteem and courage. *Thank you,* he says." I looked at the couple and added, "He is very spiritually advanced."

Then Clarke sent another thought, which I shared with the audience: "Most people with disabilities are advanced souls. Only a soul with great understanding would take on such challenges."

I thanked the couple and their cousin for coming to the show and helping to teach the rest of us.

Later, at the book signing, I was able to spend a few more moments with Scott and Linda. Scott divulged the secret to their compassionate hearts. He and Linda were middle-school teachers who loved children, and they taught some of the most challenging kids. Linda instituted specific games and sports into the school curriculum to utilize brain and motor functions to increase comprehension.

"Our kids are always the ones to get straight *A*'s," he beamed. He went on to say that many people didn't treat disabled children as humans until Linda put her programs into action. "Linda was one of the most respected and honored teachers in the school district."

I understood why. Scott and Linda had given their hearts and souls to disabled children and perhaps helped these children to feel love for the first time in their lives. It was obvious that the night had been special, and that I was in the company of some very extraordinary angels.

Time to Reincarnate

Many people ask how soon a soul reincarnates after it dies. Ten years? Two hundred years? The answer is that it is up to each individual soul. The soul makes the decision to return to earth based on the optimum factors and elements—including locating the right body, the right geographical location, the right parents, etc. Remember that time is relative on the spiritual plane. Some souls evolve rapidly; these souls tend to return more quickly than others. It is important to understand that reincarnation is not a punishment for mistakes made in a past life. It is not as if a soul must return to earth like a student returning to college for more classes. Yes, we do work out karma, but there are many light workers, evolved beings, and teachers that return to demonstrate love and compassion to others. When I first started communicating with the spirit world, I realized that spirits sometimes wait centuries before venturing back to earth. However, as the earth plane's energy begins to accelerate, souls are more eager to return because of the expanding opportunities and circumstances in which they can participate.

It is not unusual for a soul to take many earth years to plan, review its life chart, and confer with guides to decide the most opportune time to return. By the way, a soul not only factors its own chart in this decision; it also considers those soul mates with whom it will be sharing a new life experience, including parents, siblings, teachers, friends, partners, and coworkers.

As Shakespeare once wrote:

> All the world's a stage, and all the men and women merely players;
>
> They have their exits and their entrances;
>
> And one man in his time plays many parts. . . .

You may be the main player in your upcoming drama, but, in order for it to be done correctly, you must cast it perfectly and set it in an ideal place at the appropriate time so that the various scenes are played out the way you envisioned them. Depending on how good the actors are—and if they remember their lines, because there is always free will—the play may go as planned, or it may go astray. Not to worry, even if the scenery starts falling around you, be true to your part, and especially don't start reciting other people's lines. When all of the elements of a new life are set in place and a soul is aware of the upcoming potentiality, it is ready to incarnate.

The Right Time

When I was contemplating writing about reincarnation, the following story came to mind. It begins with a wonderful couple, Ann and Arnold Singer. Here, in Ann's own words, is an example of a soul waiting for the right time to return.

I knew from a very young age there would be something different about me having a child, but I couldn't understand what it was exactly. In fact, I had twenty-eight years to figure it out, because it took twenty-cight years of conventional and unconventional methods and seventeen attempts at in vitro fertilization to get pregnant. I learned to have patience in the pursuit of my goal. Twenty-eight years is a very long time to wait for a baby, but I think it really did take that long for me to learn all that I needed to learn.

First, I needed time to be in a position emotionally, financially, and spiritually, with abundant free time to give support and love to my baby at the maximum level possible. During those twenty-eight years, I developed wisdom, gratitude, and a huge depth of appreciation. I learned to be persistent. In my case, it was never give up, never give up, never give up. I learned to trust in my hopes and dreams as part of my destiny. It was my dream that kept me focused. I learned that, in order to achieve my dream, I had to learn acceptance and surrender and to be flexible in my thinking. Even though I had always been successful in everything I did in life, this was completely out of my hands. Nothing I did worked for me. I learned to live life to the fullest and to be willing to take risks and step into the void of the unknown. I learned to feel deeply and to be compassionate. Everyone has something deeply painful inside that he or she carries, and we cannot compare the pain and sorrow of one with that of another. Finally, I learned that everyone has a journey, even the baby yet to be born.

The moment I made these immense internal changes, released the idea that it had to be "my way," and accepted

the force of destiny, things changed for me in so many
ways. One day out of nowhere, I heard a voice inside: *Try
one more time.* I knew immediately that it meant trying to
have a baby. I discussed it with Arnold, and we agreed to
try one more time—and only one more time—at this late
stage in our lives. I just knew it would work this time. As
I was contemplating my decision, I had a vision of a young
man walking toward me, a princely warrior adorned in a
red cloak and shining armor. He told me his name and I
knew that this man would be my child.

In the past, there had always been difficulties with the
treatments—appointment delays, technical disruptions,
laboratory errors. There was always something amiss,
and I dreaded going through it all again. This time, it
was different; it all just flowed. Some time before the
actual conception, I saw a pair of eyes watching me in
my meditation. They were friendly and smiling, yet very
old and wise eyes. Then I could see a face and a body. He
was dressed in a long white robe, but he was not like any
person here on earth. I knew this entity was here because
of the baby. I asked this guide: What do I need to do for
this special child? He simply said: *Love him.*

Conception came in a way that I could never have
imagined and in a way that science was not able to achieve
earlier. The pregnancy was easy and uncomplicated, and
so was the birth. The baby was perfect in every way. It
came at exactly the right time both for us and for him.
A few months after the baby was born, I had a medical
appointment. It was winter and I had the baby totally
covered. As I walked through the waiting room, a young
boy about twelve years old jumped up, stood at attention,
and saluted, right there in the waiting room in front of

everyone. He said in a loud voice: "He's here. He's come back. He's come back from the future to be with us." The boy continued to stand at attention as we passed and then went back to reading his magazine. I wondered how this child knew my baby was a boy, because he was so wrapped up in blankets. The child didn't seem strange in any way and was immune to the dismissive responses from others, especially his mother. When he saw my baby, he just came alive for the moment.

This made me realize that it was the right time for this soul to be with us. We are older, we are both financially and emotionally secure, and we have all the love and time the baby needs.

Just before the baby was conceived, I had another vision of my son, at which time he told me his name. It was not a name we knew or had ever heard. We trusted my vision and named him as he told me. I have since learned that his name comes from an ancient language and means "he who has returned."

Ann was in her mid-fifties when she gave birth to her beautiful baby boy. Their son continues to grow wiser and healthier with each passing day.

The Return

It seems that, before returning to the earthly atmosphere, each soul goes before the Council of Elders or masters one last time. This Council reinforces the many lessons the soul must learn in its upcoming lifetime. In a way, these masters reaffirm the spiritual contract with the soul and instill in the soul memory the importance of getting the work done.

As Dr. Michael Newton points out in his book *Journey of Souls,* if a soul looked at the process of return from an earthly point of view, it might not return at all. It is not an easy concept to understand, but remember that everything is energy. When a soul returns through levels of dimensions, it does so as energy. Energy is made up of waves of molecules that are always in motion. At death, as a soul passes through a series of energetic realms to reenter the spiritual world, a similar transition takes place, only in reverse. A soul enters a waiting chamber, where it becomes aware of an array of light tunnels. Again, just as the soul felt drawn to the light when it left the body, it now feels influenced and inspired to return through a particular tunnel of light.

As the soul enters this tunnel, it is layered with Spirit energy that builds confidence into the soul essence. Because reentry can be confusing and upsetting for a soul, this Spirit energy helps the soul remain on course all the way through the process until birth. As this layering process takes place, the soul feels the force of human emotions heaped upon it. This is the heaviness a soul feels when entering a physical body. Think of it as putting on layers of clothing to prepare for the cold. Once all the layers of human emotion are integrated into the soul essence, the soul enters the mother's womb. Following this is the slow process of the soul's energy merging with its new physical body, which involves merging individual frequencies and patterns with the new brain. In my book *Reaching to Heaven,* I explain in detail how a soul hovers around an embryo, influencing the mother and checking on its new body—"cooking," so to speak, all of the soul's individualized ingredients into the new body.

The Valley of Forgetfulness

As a soul connects further with its newly forming physical body, the influence from the light realm lessens, and the soul goes through what is known as the Valley of Forgetfulness, also called the River Lethe (in Greek mythology, the river of forgetfulness). The word *lethe* has the same root as *lethargy,* meaning a state of sleepiness. This sleeplike state is the reason we do not remember our spiritual identities. Some say that this type of "amnesia" is a gift from God, given for two very good reasons. First, if we knew all of our past lives and the horrendous things we were capable of, we would spend all our time obsessing about the past instead of working on our current soul lessons. Second, if we knew the answer to every problem that we faced, we could not evolve spiritually. Although the soul memory may be hidden from our conscious rational minds, the soul's thought patterns are always influencing the brain to behave in a certain way. This was certainly the case when, in a recent spirit-circle demonstration, the spirit of a man surprised us with his newfound understanding. When telling of the life he had recently left, he described himself as someone who spoke with harsh criticism and judgment of others. Before his passing, he had developed throat cancer and underwent a laryngectomy. The operation left a noticeable scar across his throat. He surprised us all when he communicated this insight: *Words have power, and when I return to my next life, I will keep the scar to remind me to speak with love and respect.*

As the soul checks in and out of its body, it continues to connect with brain-wave patterns, making sure its body is growing according to plan. A soul will not enter the fetus until the final months of the pregnancy—and even then, it can and will exit the body up to three months after birth. The soul gently melds with the mind, expanding its memory through the entire body. In the meantime, it relaxes the physical body of the child, while determining a course of action after birth. By the age of six, the passage into the Valley of Forgetfulness is complete, and the child no longer remembers its spiritual origins.

The last part of this book focuses on how parents and children connect. It gives ways we can heal the pain and grief of losing a child, and considers how love never dies. In the next chapter, I describe how children contact their parents and loved ones.

PART THREE

Healing Your Life

7

Spirit Signposts

*If you could only keep quiet, clear of
memories and expectations, you would be
able to discern the beautiful pattern of events.
It's your restlessness that causes chaos.*

—SRI NISARGADATTA MAHARAJ

THROUGH YEARS OF INTERACTING with the other side of life, I have found that spirits are constantly attempting to contact the living. The most obvious way is through thought. Almost always, the moment your loved one comes to mind is the moment when your loved one is nearby. Usually, a spirit will project a thought to your mind. You may think: I wonder how my daughter is? In reality, you are picking up the transmission of her thought. I often say to my audiences: "How many of you have had thoughts about your spirit family fill your head when you are driving your car or making dinner?" Every person in the audience raises his or her hand; most have had this type of experience at least once. Spirits will try every way possible to let you know that they are still very much a part of your life.

Every person is born with a sixth sense, or intuition, but most don't use it. Intuition means "language of the soul." Our souls communicate directly to us through this sixth sense of intuition. When you listen to your intuition, you become much more aware of the spirititual world. As you become more sensitized to this sixth sense, you will know when your loved one is around you. As a medium, I have sharpened my intuitive sixth sense from years of practice and daily meditation. We are all electromagnetic beings, so we all speak the same language.

Meditation

Most people pray, which is a form of asking for something. Meditation, on the other hand, is a form of listening. Meditation is like contemplation. It is a focused state of consciousness or concentration. Most of us breeze through the day, sometimes totally unaware of what is happening around us. Our minds wander; we're either thinking of the future or reliving the past. We're really not living in the present moment. Just think of the times when you watched TV or a movie, and you missed some important dialogue. You may have been watching, but your mind was off somewhere else. Thank goodness for DVRs and DVDs, because we can just rewind and replay. The same can be said for reading a book, or even cooking. (Did I put that ingredient in or not?) As energetic beings, we are all on various levels of consciousness throughout the day.

When you meditate, you focus your mind to behave in the way you instruct it. You concentrate on your breath, or on a word or phrase. Whenever your mind wanders, you return to the breath, word, or phrase. The main point of any meditation is to be mindful of what is going on around you and within you. Mindful meditation is the art of becoming deeply aware of the present situation. Think of it as a mental clearing; you are letting go of all thoughts as they pass through your mind, because you stay focused on that single word, phrase, or breath. Try it for a minute. Sit quietly and concentrate on your breath. You will begin to feel a complete stillness around you and within you. The spirit world is able to get through to you easily when your mind is still and clear. Meditation is often referred to as "sitting in the silence." Whenever you want to reach Spirit from this side of life, start by sitting in the silence.

I always include a meditation in my demonstrations and workshops. I find this very important for two distinct reasons. First, it puts the audience members at ease. Some may have come to the event with preconceived notions, fears, expectations, and negativity. Second, meditation raises our vibration, and we become closer to the vibration of the spirit world, which makes it easier for spirits to come through. Think of spirit contact as trying to land a plane in the dark. When you meditate, it's as if you turn on the runway lights.

In order to get the best result from meditation, it is important to set aside a room or portion of a room, and a time of the day when you will not be disturbed. Be consistent. You are not only making an appointment for yourself, you are putting the spirit world on notice that this is the time to be together. Being consistent causes a problem for a lot of people. I can only say that, if you are dedicated, it is worth it. Also, be aware that your mind is going to chatter. Don't sit and judge the chatter; just realize that it will be part of the experience and let it be. The more you judge something, the more you stay stuck in it. It's like floating down a river; if you get caught on the rocks, move aside and keep going.

Rainbow Bridge Meditation

It is impossible for me to give a message to everyone in a large audience; therefore, I have devised many meditations for individuals to use on their own time. The following meditation is great for making contact and receiving signs from a loved one.

Find a room or place where you will not be disturbed for at least fifteen minutes. Make sure it is a quiet, well-ventilated room, and that you are sitting in a comfortable chair with your back straight against the chair. You may have some soft, gentle music playing in the background; it should be something that won't disturb your experience. Set your atmosphere for an optimum encounter. Close the windows and turn off TVs, cell phones, and any other noise-making distractions. It is very helpful to have a pad and pen available so that you can write down any insights, messages, or signs that the spirit gives you.

Start by closing your eyes and focusing on your body. Acknowledge each part of your body, beginning at the head and going through the rest—neck, shoulders, back, arms, hands, chest, stomach, legs—ending at your feet. When this is completed, focus your awareness on your breathing, one breath at a time. Imagine a beam of gold light coming into your body from the cosmos far, far above you. The gold beam (or, as I like to say, the "God beam") comes into your body through the top of your head with each inhalation. As you inhale, imagine this gold light filling you up and blending into each cell of your body, illuminating every muscle, blood vessel, and organ. Spirit is light, and the idea here is to raise your vibration to be as close as you can to that level of light. To do this, you have to release the heavier parts held within. As you exhale, imagine dark energy flowing out from your fingertips and toes, falling onto the earth. Mother Earth absorbs this dark energy and transforms it into love.

With each breath, the gold light fills you up and any old energy or debris you no longer need to carry around with you is released. After several cleansing breaths, imagine the gold light coming back out the top of your head, swirling around on top of you, and forming a rainbow of colors—red, orange, yellow, green, blue, purple, indigo, and gold. Each color has a specific vibration of energy, so feel and experience the value and characteristic of each color. After several minutes of the swirling rainbow, see the colors going back to the cosmos. Imagine them going to a faraway space; in that space, your rainbow colors begin to create a bridge. It is a very special bridge made of your own rainbow light. Create every detail of the bridge, right down to the suspension and pavement. When the bridge begins to glisten, your creation is finished.

Now begin to walk upon your bridge. There may be some mist there; just walk through it. As you get to the center of this glistening, illuminated bridge, you will begin to see the spirits of the people who have passed to the higher life standing before you. They have projected themselves so that you can have an experience with them. It is real. As you go to hug them, feel their energy and their personalities. You can even talk to them and ask them questions. You will be surprised by what they have to say, but don't judge it. Just enjoy the experience and listen with your heart. They may tell you what to look or listen for in the future to let you know that they are around you. You may not be able to see them, but you can feel their energy. That is okay, too. Receive the energy however it is presented. You may want to write down what they share with you.

When you have finished your journey, once again place your focus on your feet and the rest of your body. Move your attention from your feet up through your legs, midsection, stomach, chest, shoulders, neck, and back, to your head. You probably feel a difference in your body. You may notice that something has shifted in your body. This meditation is a wonderful tool for healing the body, mind, and spirit.

Dreams

Spirits constantly want to interact with us, and some are better at communicating than others. One of the more successful ways they let us know they are around is through our dreams. This is the most common method used by spirit children to give us messages. Dreams work for a number of reasons. First, we are in a subconscious state, and the rational, judgmental part of the mind is temporarily suspended. Therefore, we are more receptive to the unseen dimensions and can merge more easily with the soul energy of those who have passed over. Second, during sleep, our spirit bodies leave the encasement of our physical bodies and travel in the astral world. This is known as astral travel. In the astral world, we can connect with our deceased loved ones, and our spirit guides and soul group. All of us have experienced dreams of deceased loved ones. I call these dreams "crossovers" because they seem so very real. The colors are vivid; loved ones behave in a normal fashion; and, unlike ordinary dreams, the dream events happen in chronological order, as if we have stepped into a slice of life.

I often get messages in dreams from my deceased family and friends. In the early nineties, I lost a very close friend named John. He was a true soul mate and mentor to me during my life in Los Angeles. A schoolteacher in Fort Lauderdale, John visited me during school breaks and summer vacation. We spent hours, sometimes days, talking about my psychic abilities and metaphysical subjects. John was a bit skeptical when I told him of my soon-to-be career as a medium. He had a wicked sense of humor and promised to haunt me when he was dead. Several months after he passed, he came to me in one of the most vivid dreams of my life.

I was just getting up when John called me into the kitchen for breakfast. Both of us were wearing bathrobes, and I was sitting at the table watching him turn the eggs over in a pan on the stove. I remember questioning the reality of the dream, and he jokingly said: "I had to create it this way because it's the only way you would believe I am with you." He then asked me, "What kind of tea would you like?" It seemed so real, because this was the same way we interacted every time he came for a visit. When he opened the cupboard, I could clearly see the packet of each tea bag, right down to the foil pouch. I picked a tea called Fortitude, and then I woke up. Later that day, as I recalled every aspect of the dream, I realized that John was trying to help me get over his death, which had been very hard for me. All I needed was exactly what he was serving—a little bit of fortitude.

I received another vivid dream message about ten years ago from my mother. Although she had been deceased for some time, in the dream I found myself at her wake. I was kneeling before her coffin saying prayers and feeling very badly that she had died. I got up, turned around, and started to walk away. As I turned back to look at her one last time, she popped up in the coffin like a jack-in-the-box. She sat there and laughed at me. I was completely shocked and distraught. As soon as I woke up, I realized that my mother was trying to pass along the message that she was not dead and that it was silly to think that anybody really dies.

Electrical Energy

Electricity is another very common method used by spirits to contact us. Because everything is made up of electromagnetic energy, spirits are able to focus their thoughts to manipulate the electromagnetic field around various electrical objects. In this way, they are able to turn on or off anything that utilizes electricity—appliances, lights, televisions, computers, radios, microwaves, ovens, cell phones, cars, garage doors, street-lights, doorbells, and more. Some things are easier to manipulate than others. Or a spirit may have a working knowledge of a certain item. Many times, spirits manipulate the radio to impress a loved one with a special song. I have had several people come to me at a book signing or workshop and tell me that, suddenly, in the middle of the night while they were sleeping, the television popped on displaying a repeat of my daytime syndicated show *Beyond*. They knew at that moment that it was a sign from their deceased loved one that they should pay attention. Interestingly, many people have said that the particular segment of the show they were shown was about a death situation similar to the one experienced by the loved one. Spirits are known to burn out lights and mess with cameras and recorders. They are also notorious for draining battery life. I cannot tell you how many times I have had to warn the audio crew on a television shoot to keep extra batteries on hand. Often, as many as eight batteries have been needed for a one-hour show.

Clairalience and Cold Spots

Smelling aromas—perfume, fresh flowers, cigarettes, pipe tobacco, or aftershave lotion—when they are not physically present is a mediumistic phenomenon called "clairalience." Spirits can and do project these scents to get our attention, and these smells are usually directly related to them. One client told me that she knows her son is around when the aroma of freshly popped popcorn fills a room, because he made fresh popcorn at least once a week. Another woman said that she smelled her daughter's favorite perfume in the house every week for a year after she passed over. Both women were comforted to know that their children were still around.

Another sign that a spirit is close at hand is the experience of chills or cold spots in a room, even when the heat is on. Over the years, the phenomenon of cold spots has been a recurring theme during my spiritual development circles. It is not uncommon for participants to sense half their bodies becoming cold as spirits enter the circle. I have had letters from many parents who have told me that, when they sit on their child's bed, they get the chills.

Photographs, Likenesses, and Words

Photography is a popular way for spirits to make themselves known, although it is not as easy as you may think. There are many elements to consider for a spirit to impress itself in a photograph—atmospheric conditions, its ability to concentrate thought at a very low frequency, projecting its energy to the magnetism of the camera, and the mind of the photographer. Sometimes the photographer may have some undeveloped mediumship capabilities that a spirit can utilize to manifest on a picture. When a spirit attempts this type of communication, it can display either its face or its entire body.

Depending on circumstances and conditions, spirits have been known to project their energy to appear as spheres of light. These orbs, as they are called, can vary in size, shape, color, and mass. When I was in Washington recently with my friend Joerdie, we visited the Ford Theater where Lincoln was assassinated. I remember sitting in the balcony and inviting my spirit friends and guides to come close to me. Then I asked Joerdie to take my picture. A great many orbs manifested on the photo. We were amazed, but I knew that Joerdie is extremely mediumistic in her own right.

Spirits can also send a sign by impressing their likeness on a living person. You may be on a plane, in a store, or even walking down the street, when you are suddenly moved to look at a certain person who appears to have an uncanny resemblance to your loved one. This has happened to me so many times at demonstrations. As I look out to the audience, I inevitably see several people who look exactly like family and friends of mine in the spirit world.

Another common sign is given through words. Someone may use a word or phrase that your deceased loved one once used in exactly the same way. My mother's sign was the phrase "blue moon." I cannot tell you how many times this phrase has popped up in conversations where it didn't have anything to do with what was being discussed, or was very far removed from what a person would normally say.

Apports and Animal Signs

How many times have you misplaced your car keys or wallet? When you find them, you wonder how they got there. For years, this happened to me, until a psychic finally shed some light on the mystery, telling me that I had some mischievous children spirits who played at hiding things from me. In mediumship lingo, this is known as "apports," or objects dematerializing in one place and materializing in another. Moving objects is difficult to do, so a spirit has to develop and regularly practice this ability to be effective.

Spirits use animals and other creatures as well to communicate with us. Have you ever seen a butterfly, a bird, or a dragonfly and thought that your son or daughter was giving you a sign that they were near you? This is one of the most popular questions I am asked. Here is my understanding of how this phenomena works. A spirit may be next to you and project a thought of itself to you at the exact time you see a butterfly, bird, or dragonfly. Immediately, you associate the bird or insect with your loved one. So in a way, you could say that the creature *is* your loved one. I also know that a spirit is capable of manipulating the flight of a bird or butterfly.

A woman wrote to me about her baby girl who had passed at four weeks of age. "The only time I am okay is when I get little signs from her. I was feeling sad and went to the cemetery to be near her. I told her that I hoped she had met my grandparents, because they were wonderful. As I was placing roses on her grave, I saw this beautiful ladybug among the flowers that were there. It's cold and rainy where I live, so I knew it was way past ladybug season. Ladybugs were my grandma's favorite and, before she passed, she told me to look for them as a sign from her. It brought a bit of light to my day. I can imagine them (my grandparents) holding my little one and spoiling her rotten over there."

One day after my friend Joan's husband passed, she received a sign from him while she was driving on the freeway. A dragonfly perched on the outside mirror and remained there for half an hour. She thought it was a pretty amazing sign, as she and her husband shared a love of dragonflies. Spirits also use our pets to communicate. Sometimes you may see a cat staring into space or meowing over nothing. One mother wrote about how her son Raymond, who died in a car accident, plays with his pet. "He visits with his dog. She will suddenly madly wag her tail and, even though she's getting to be an old girl, she plops down on her front legs and is ready to play. He used to play with her in the stairwell. Now, when she lies at the top of the stairs barking at the staircase and wagging her tail, we know Ray has come to see her."

Symbols

Spirits can use any sort of sign or symbol to impress us with their presence. I remember very distinctly the time I drove through upstate New York on my way to visit my mother's hometown. As I drove on the thruway, I wondered if my mother knew that I was a medium. She died before I became involved in my present line of work. Suddenly, an eighteen-wheeler switched lanes right in front of me. I was startled to see the name of the company, McLane, on the truck. It was my mother's maiden name. I looked heavenward and said, Thank you!

My friend Joerdie has been having manifestations from her son, Ian, since he passed over in 1997. She called me the other day and, during our hour-long conversation, she cried: "Oh my gosh, you are never going to believe what just happened!" She noticed moisture accumulating between the panes of the window and, as she looked closer, letters began to develop. First an I, then an A, and finally an N. She started laughing, then looked up to heaven and jokingly yelled to her son: "Ah ha! What else do you have?" At that remark, a heart formed next to the letters. This same sign appeared five more times with even more embellishment. How else can a son tell you he loves you?

Spirits can use bumper stickers, billboards, ads on a subway station wall, magazines, newspaper headlines, and all sorts of ways to get a message across. If you do not get signs from your loved ones, don't worry. There is a lot going on for children in heaven. But rest assured, they will contact you in some form or another.

An Exceptional Student

The following story is from a woman who attended my demonstration in Toronto. She wrote to me about an incredible sign she had received from someone she least expected.

Dear James,

I've been meaning to write to you these last few years. During a session you held in Toronto, you focused on a family who had lost their child. These people sat a few seats from my daughter and me. Suddenly, you asked this family, "Who is Susie?" Nobody recognized the name, and you continued. I did not want to interrupt you and say the message could be for me. I have always wondered, however, what Susie might have said if I had responded.

Let me explain about Susie. I am a retired elementary school teacher, and Susie was a very special student. She suffered from a severe form of Cerebral Palsy. She was totally incapacitated, and was fed through a tube. Susie was adopted by a worker in the hospital and became an important member of their family. Susie was integrated into the regular classroom and, to me, she was just another student. It never occurred to me that she might die.

Susie's educational assistant and I encouraged the other students to interact with her. They read books to her and shared stories and pictures. Listening to them made Susie happy and brought forth smiles and giggles. She became especially animated during music class. Susie moved on through the grades, but her assistant often brought her back into my class during our daily music sessions. She brought out the best in other students, and certain children dedicated their recess times to be with her.

During the summer of 2002, we had very little rainfall, and my daughter and I were concerned that our cistern would run dry. One Saturday in July, a thunderstorm developed and, before retiring, we expressed our desire to have lots of rain to carry us through. The next morning, my daughter asked if I had checked the cistern. I told her the cement lid was too heavy and had to be pried off. She was very perplexed, as the lid had already been lifted off and pushed aside. There was no way this could have just happened by itself. I explained it away, saying that perhaps lightning had hit the lid, causing it to pop up. My daughter put the lid back in place that morning.

At noon, my daughter and I were on the patio discussing this strange event, when I just happened to glance at the cistern. "Did the lid look like that?" I noticed that the lid was pushed out and up. My daughter was shocked. "Did you do that?" she asked. "No, I didn't touch it."

The following Monday, I learned that Susie had passed away. She was fifteen years old and had been in a coma over the weekend. When I went to the funeral home,

I was surprised to see a school photo of Susie and my second-grade class on display.

I have always felt that Susie must have been responsible for moving the cistern lid and wanted to communicate to me that, in spirit, she had the strength to overcome all obstacles. The following year, when you asked, "Who is Susie?" it helped to confirm the fact that Susie had been trying to contact me. I wish you all the best.

Sincerely,
Clarice

Numbers

My good friend Marilyn Whall is a medium who went on tour with me through the United Kingdom. As we drove through a town one evening, she called my attention to a car with a series of numbers on it. "If numbers are repeated three times, like that 222 over there," she said, "everything will be all right. 333 means a connection with the Ascended Masters." She went on to tell me that she had learned about numbers from another good friend of mine, angel practitioner Doreen Virtue. I laughed and told her of a fabulous lunch I had with Doreen. We were headed to our restaurant and stopped at a red light. She immediately looked at the license plate of the car in front of us, which contained the number 444. Doreen immediately said: "The angels are all around us!" This fascinated me, and I wanted to learn more about the messages in numbers. Doreen had written a book entitled *Healing with the Angels.* that contains a section on the meaning of numbers, repeated numbers, and numbers in sequence. Here is some food for thought from her book:

111: There is a gate of opportunity opening up, and your thoughts are manifesting into form at record speed.

222: Don't worry about anything as the situation is resolving itself beautifully for everyone involved.

333: The Ascended Masters are near you, desiring you to know that you have their help, love, and companionship.

444: Thousands of angels surround you at this moment, loving and supporting you.

555: A major life change is upon you.

666: Your thoughts are out of balance right now, focused too much on the material world.

777: Keep up the good work and know your wish is coming true.

888: You are winding up an emotional career or relationship phase. It also means there is light at the end of the tunnel.

999: Get to work, light worker! The world needs your divine life purpose right now.

000: A reminder you are one with God. In addition, it is a sign that a situation has gone full circle.

His Favorite Number

Usually, I begin my seminars with some "ghostly" humor to relax the crowd. Laughter helps to calm the tension and raise the vibratory energy in the room. Then I ask participants to close their eyes and guide them through a meditation. The meditation usually ends with a visualization in which they meet spirit loved ones. In 2010, as I hosted this type of demonstration in Oregon, several powerful and emotional readings came through—one especially about a young teen who died of leukemia. The following is a portion of a letter sent from his mother, who attended the demonstration.

Dear James,

My son, Dan, passed away when he was nineteen. After he passed, I could not stand not being able to guide him. A parent is supposed to die before her child. I hated not knowing if he was all right. Many times, I would ask him for a sign—a song on the radio or the number 44 (his football number). Most of the time, the sign appeared. My logical side kept nagging me that it was all coincidence or that the signs appeared because I was looking for them.

Not long after Dan passed, a friend mentioned that she was reading a book by you that she thought I might like. Before I knew it, I had read three more of your books. I saw that you were coming to Oregon and I asked my friend to purchase tickets. I immediately told my son that I was going to see you and asked him to do his best to be there.

At the seminar, you smiled and told us to quit begging for our spirits to visit, because they were already chosen. Toward the end of the meditation, I saw Dan and felt such an overwhelming sense of warmth and love. The floodgates opened. I could feel the tears hit my chest. It was like nothing I had ever experienced. Then the spirits began presenting themselves. The fourth spirit came through. It never occurred to me that it would be Dan. Number 44 was huge to my son.

You relayed, "There is a mom in the audience and her son, who is around eighteen or nineteen years old, is here."

My heart stopped, and my mind went blank.

"He is showing me car decals and personalized license plates."

That message was for me! How did he know? The tickets were not in my name. I raised my hand.

"Thank you," you said.

"Your son died one or two years ago. He touched a lot of people in his life."

I nodded. Dan did touch a lot of people. When we had his service at the high school football stadium, 900 people were in attendance. The school retired his number-44 jersey.

"Your son went to Hawaii to learn how to surf. Do you understand?"

"Yes." What I needed to hear. Dan loved Hawaii. "How is he?" I asked.

You responded with a smile. "Mom, he is fine. He is surfing and having lots of fun."

I felt so relieved.

You continued. "Your son could not stop what happened."

I knew we had done everything possible, but there was always that thought, "what if."

"He is showing me a tattoo on your arm with his name. Your son is saying that he really likes the tattoo."

I got a tattoo on the inside of my wrist with Dan's signature and an infinity symbol. I knew he would like it. Dan wanted a tattoo on his arm, too.

"Your son is very loving and an old soul."

Dan was incredibly loving. He wanted everyone to be happy.

"There is a football helmet in your son's room. He is showing me all the signatures on the helmet. You go into his room a lot and look at the helmet."

I do look at it often.

"This spirit is watching over his brother and is with him all the time."

The week before, my younger son said someone was watching over him.

You looked at me and smiled. "Your son has been waiting a long time to talk to you."

I smiled. That was Dan. Impatient.

"Your son is saying that, on earth, he was afraid to die, but he isn't afraid anymore."

Words I needed to hear.

There was so much shared, and this is only some of it. Everything you said had an impact. There was information that I didn't understand during the seminar, but after asking people, I found that it was accurate.

James, your reading gave me peace. I no longer have the uncontrollable desire to protect and guide Dan. I know Dan is with me and, when it is my time to transition, Dan will be there waiting for me. In the meantime, I have a life to live; I have to be the best mom for my younger son.

Thank you, James, for an incredible gift of peace.

Evelyn

Synchronicity and Coincidence

I often tell clients that we are puppets, and spirits are the puppet masters and influencing our experiences for our greatest good. Here is an example of synchronicity: You are reading an obscure word in a book at the very same instant you hear it spoken on TV; later that day, you hear the same word used in conversation by someone you know. Unless the word holds some personal or symbolic meaning, such a synchronicity will likely leave you wondering. But it will also make you aware of something special at work.

When we are aware that consciousness is limitless, we are able to raise our energy vibration and begin to experience synchronicity as a regular occurrence. We understand that nothing is coincidental, that accidents don't happen, and that we are not always in control of circumstances and events (even though we think we ought to be). I think this is a sign from Spirit telling us that we are correctly in the flow of universal energy and on the path that is intended for us.

Like synchronicity, coincidences sometimes seem unimportant. These quirky happenstances often appear as small glitches in the fabric of our reality. They seem to offer no significance other than alerting us to the fact that there is more going on regarding our physical experience than meets the eye.

Is It a Coincidence?

Here is a very interesting story that seems to tie in very nicely with my point about coincidences. About sixteen years ago, I was living in a small one-bedroom apartment in Hollywood doing two readings a day. The first was a ninety-minute session that began at eleven. I finished my meditation in preparation for this first session, double-checked the tape recorder and reached for the pad that I always kept on a table next to my chair. The doorbell rang, and I ran down the stairs to answer it. I opened the door to find Jerry, an average, middle-aged man.

I invited Jerry inside and offered him a glass of water. After handing him the water, I ushered him into my sitting room. Jerry took a seat directly in front of me, and I explained how the process of spirit communication worked. I told him that I always insisted on keeping the identity of the person the client wanted to contact secret. In this way, I could be sure that no one other than Spirit and my guides could direct the session.

Twenty minutes into the session, the air in the room suddenly shifted. This happened because the spirit had changed, changing the energy as a result. I became aware of a piano keyboard above my client's head, and the figure of a man playing it. I did not see a face, but clearly heard the spirit say in a light but direct voice: *Tell him it is Lee. He knows me!*

I explained my impressions, and Jerry was shocked. "That's Liberace! I wondered if he would show up. As a matter of fact, when I was at the drugstore to buy the cassette tape, I had a thought that maybe he would."

I was also shocked. I had been somewhat familiar with Liberace, as I had seen some of his television specials years before. I must say that I was always in awe of his style and how he captivated audiences with his outlandish costumes and over-the-top flamboyance.

That day, Lee was a strong communicator. I recall how very upset he was, and how concerned that certain items of his estate were being mishandled. It seemed that some of his wishes were not being carried out. He was angry that the people he had trusted only seemed interested in grabbing some of his wealth for themselves. The reading ended, and I did not think about it again until I began thinking about coincidences.

Fast forward to a year ago. I purchased a house in Palm Springs very close to Liberace's former residence, which he called The Cloisters. I remember seeing his signature seven-foot candelabra in the front yard, and the letter "L" inscribed in wrought iron on each of the windows. Every time I passed his house, I wondered what it had been like when he lived there. A few months ago, I drove by and noticed that its new owners were gutting the house. I was sad to see that they were taking away most of what was once a very special home.

While writing this book, I was in Las Vegas doing an event. My assistant Christy and I happened to drive right by the Liberace Museum. I had heard a lot about the place, but had never had a chance to visit. I asked Christy to stop so we could take a look inside. We pulled into the shopping-center parking lot, and I got out of the car. I began to sense a strange feeling of nostalgia as I tried opening the door. Unfortunately, it was locked, and again I felt sad. I turned back to Christy, who was waiting in the car. Immediately, a pickup truck pulled up beside me.

The driver, a man with long white hair, yelled out "It's closed! They closed it on the seventeenth." He then went into a tirade about how the person in charge of the foundation allegedly embezzled all the funds and sold all the cars, coats, hats, and valuable memorabilia, using the proceeds for his own greedy purposes. This gentleman, Bill, was very upset. "I used to work for Lee. He was a nice guy, and it's a shame how his things ended up." I noticed a woman (his wife) next to him. She was paging through a magazine and acknowledging everything her husband said.

"I would love to have seen the museum," I said.

"Do you want to see Liberace's first house here in Vegas?"

"Sure!" I jumped into the car, and we followed Bill. It took us about ten minutes to get to the location. The house was vacant and only remnants of days gone by remained. There was a tattered piano-keyboard awning over the side door, and the famous "L" on the iron fence. Bill said that he had built the cabinetry in the house, as well as the stained-glass windows. Once again, a feeling of nostalgia hit me, and I felt as if I had lost out on something special. I was thankful that Bill and his wife just "happened" to drive up at the exact time I was in the parking lot. Without them, I would never have seen Liberace's house or learned the backstory of his life. A week passed, and I started to review the whole scenario in my head. I wondered if Liberace in spirit had maneuvered these events. It didn't take long to find out.

The next weekend, I was on my way to Phoenix for a conference entitled *Celebrate Your Life.* On the plane, I reached into my briefcase for a book. (I always keep several books with me, and go from one to the other, never sure which one I will pick.) This time, I pulled out *The Biography of Liberace.* I was surprised. I opened the book and started reading. "We had saved up enough money for Lee to open his own museum . . ." Wow! I was blown away! My assistant and her husband, David, picked me up, and we drove to a restaurant for dinner. After I finished telling them the story about what had happened with the Liberace book, my iPhone started to play. It was so weird, because the phone had been turned off when I was on the plane. I looked at the phone to see what was playing. The title of the song was "I Got the Message" by the band Men Without Hats.

Some of you may think that what happened was just a series of coincidences, but that is exactly how the spirit world contacts us. It was obvious to me that all these circumstances came together in a synchronistic way to say a few words about Liberace. If I felt sad for this man, there are many who knew him that must have felt just as sad.

In the next chapter on grief, I will talk more about sadness, how to deal with emotions, and how to let go and move on.

8

Moving On

We cannot cure the world of sorrows,
but we can choose to live in joy.

—JOSEPH CAMPBELL

DECEASED CHILDREN do not want their parents to feel sad. They want them to move on with life in the best possible way. That said, the loss of a child causes a parent to feel unbearable guilt, blame, doubt, fear, and anguish. No words are enough; no hugs are enough. Nothing seems enough to console a parent. Grieving parents are different from others who are grieving. All expectations for a normal life are shattered for them. It is the most painful experience imaginable, and there is no quick fix. It takes time, love, and effort to move forward, so patience, above all, is essential.

In order to take the first step toward any kind of normal life, parents must acknowledge the tragedy of their loss, and they must believe they can heal. So often, parents tell me that they can't go on living, and there are some parents who don't physically make it. However, most parents survive and move on with their lives. Grieving is a process that is not like anything we have ever felt. We are not taught what it is and how to do it. That is why so many people feel lost and alone as they grieve.

Although there is no set way for someone to grieve the loss of a child, there are healthy ways to go through the process. One of the most valuable insights I can share is to remind you to attempt, as best as you can, to place yourself in a state of mindfulness. It is important not only to be aware of yourself as a spiritual, energetic being, but also to live that way every day. This may be a very difficult task, because life has become so hectic and immediate. When I suggest that people take thirty minutes a day to meditate, I get looks that tell me I am out of my mind. How can anyone find that much time to meditate? Unfortunately, far too many people pay more attention to how others perceive them than to who they are. We seem to spend more time reacting to others than we do accepting ourselves and living fully in our own truth. After a while, it can get very tiring trying to live up to someone else's perception of who we are and what we should be.

This is also true for the grieving process. Never let anyone else tell you how to or how long you should grieve. You are a unique being and no two people grieve the same way; everyone feels different things at different times. Remember, too, that energy flows up and down your spine all the time. When you don't process your feelings, emotional upset stays inside you, plugging up your emotional centers. When your energy is stuck and can't flow up and down your body easily, it can turn into dis-ease.

Stages of Grieving

Your child is gone, and numbness descends upon you like a dark shroud. You think: It can't be true; I must be dreaming.

Myriad feelings float over you in waves, and your mind tries to make sense of the unthinkable. Even with family and friends around, you feel utterly alone. You have entered the first stage of grief: shock, denial, and isolation. In my book *Healing Grief,* I describe these stages of grieving in detail. In the beginning, you feel overwhelmed, and your body may respond to your feelings with sleepless nights and loss of appetite. Or the opposite may occur—you may sleep all day and overeat from stress. Shock and denial act as defense mechanisms for the conscious mind, because facing the truth seems almost impossible. Denial is like a Band-Aid on a gunshot wound, but some parents tend to stay in denial for a while, distracting themselves with chores, work, and other forms of busyness. Many people are quite good at compartmentalizing their lives and separating their feelings from daily activities. Even though you don't want to feel anything, the healthy solution is to feel the hurt and pain. Once you are able to acknowledge to yourself that your child is gone from this earthly life, then you can accept that your child is very real in Spirit and is close to you as long as need be.

After you are able to admit that your child is gone, the next stage is usually anger. You are angry with yourself, your spouse, your life, God, your belief in goodness, and more. You are angry at the world. How could God take my beautiful child? What did I do to deserve this? Why couldn't I die instead? I remember talking to a woman on a radio show who was very distraught about her son's death from cancer. She did not want to face that he was gone, yet she was very angry with God for taking him from her. The first thing I said was, "It's good that you are talking about your son." She was surprised and taken aback. I went on to tell her: "Your son is right here and he is saying that he's all right. He's not in pain anymore. He is saying, *I am free.*"

The woman began to sob and couldn't talk, so the radio host had to move on to the next caller. I slipped the host a note requesting to speak with the woman after the show. When I called her back, she sounded much calmer. "Thank you, James," she said. "I've been holding in the pain for so long. I was mad at the world, and hearing you tell me that my son was free just broke through whatever barrier I had around me." I was glad to hear that she could finally get in touch with her feelings. "Your son is still around you," I told her. "He's been waiting for you to open up so he could communicate with you." Immediately, she said, "Yes, I understand. I can see that I couldn't let him or anyone else into my heart."

Unfortunately, anger not only keeps the spirit world out, it also keeps other people away—especially other children in the house. Often, children, not completely understanding death, blame themselves—they think they did something wrong, or that they are not as good as the brother or sister who died. Even young children know that something is wrong and go through some sort of grief. No one, especially a child, wants to face an angry person. There are many ways to let anger out safely, but please don't aim it at those nearest and dearest to you. Holding on to anger and bitterness certainly blocks your energy flow. I have heard from many readers about people who develop a terminal illness within a year of losing someone. One woman wrote and told me that her husband was so devastated by their son's death that he, too, left the world soon after.

The next stage in grieving is guilt, resentment, and blame. It must be my fault. Or it must be your fault. These feelings are extremely common in parents of deceased children. After all, parents are supposed to protect their children, so somewhere, somehow, they feel they have failed in their duty. The death of a child creates a great deal of resentment and blame between parents, and I have seen far too many couples get divorced after a child dies. I remember doing a reading many years ago in my home in Los Angeles for a mother whose daughter was killed in a boating accident. She told me that she separated from her husband because she blamed him for giving her daughter permission to go sailing with her teenage friends, who were drinking onboard the boat. She kept saying: "It was his fault. If he hadn't let her go, she would still be alive today."

Her feelings of blame had more to do with control than grief. I explained that she could not control her daughter's activities any more than she could control the weather. When her daughter came through in spirit, she begged her mother to forgive her father, and the woman broke down and cried like a baby. *It's not Dad's fault. You have to stay together.* The spirit was quite insistent. Then the daughter said something that made the hair on the back of my neck stand up: *My sisters will not make it without the both of you. They will turn to drugs and die like me.* Hearing this, the mother sat straight up, wiped away her tears, and looked into my eyes. "Oh, my God. We can't desert our two little girls." Thankfully, the woman reconciled with her husband, and the family has thrived.

As with any stage of grief, there is no timeline or time limit. How long it takes to go through each step of the process is up to each individual. Some people may take months; some may go in and out of grief for a year, or for many years. The key is to go through your feelings until you reach an acceptance of what has happened, and understand that your child is in heaven watching over you. If you can accept this in your heart, then you are on your way to moving on with your life.

That said, many parents stay in negative reactions and feelings like anger, guilt, and blame for far too long. Stuck in their inability to cope with their loss, they can become depressed and morose. Often, depression leads to overuse or abuse of drugs and alcohol to numb the painful feelings. Bad behavior can sometimes follow the loss of a child. Men, especially, tend to act out what they are not able to express. Some shut down totally and will not talk to anyone. They go through the motions of living, but are dead inside. Some may start drinking; others may behave in a way totally opposite to the way they usually would. Women may also behave very differently than they once did by not taking care of themselves, not eating, not getting out of bed, or not getting dressed. Then there are those who are so depressed that they have suicidal thoughts. When depression and bad behavior take over your life, please seek professional help.

Sense of Purpose

The death of your child is an ending of one part of your life, but also the beginning of another. Grieving is a sort of purification process that helps you move on to the next part of your journey. Healthy grief means dealing with emotions; unhealthy grief means masking or numbing emotions. There are a variety of ways to say good-bye to your child. Letter writing is one. Usually, I have participants in my classes write letters to their children. I will explain how in detail in the next chapter, *Letters from Heaven*. Journal writing is another way to express your feelings. Talking to your loved one through meditation and prayer can also open your senses to let you receive messages in return.

As you say good-bye, let go of the beliefs and feelings that you have been harboring—all the what-ifs that have run through your mind over and over again. Replace these self-sabotaging thoughts with positive ones. Even if you have trouble controlling your negative thoughts, you can neutralize them with positive words. When you fear something, you block anything else from coming to you. Gradually replace your fears, negative thoughts, and disturbing feelings with something better. I'm not saying that any of this is easy, but remember that your child had a mission to fulfill on this earthly place, and you have one, too.

Once you are able to accept what has happened, forgive yourself and forgive your child. Forgive your spouse, your partner, and any other person in your life. Forgiveness is an act of grace and compassion. Everyone can benefit from it. Acceptance and forgiveness allow us to start a new chapter in our lives and clear the space for new opportunities to reach us. Your child has given you a gift—and perhaps a new purpose in life. It is up to you to fulfill your soul's purpose and mission in life.

Forgiveness Meditation

I would like to share with you a forgiveness meditation that Spirit gave me one day while I was teaching a class at the Omega Institute. When I do a meditation with my class, I always know beforehand what the focus will be, but I am never sure how Spirit will get me there. I simply open my senses and let my mind blend with Spirit, and the words flow out as if someone else were speaking. So, if you are still holding on to resentment and bitterness, try this meditation. You may be very pleased with the results.

Find a quiet place where you will not be disturbed for at least a half hour. Make sure you are away from any outside disturbances like phones, TVs, people's voices, etc. It is important that you sit in a comfortable chair with your back straight. I prefer to sit in darkness, to be totally immersed in the meditation. You may prefer to play some soothing spiritual music in the background, or not. Closing your eyes also helps you focus inwardly.

Next, concentrate on the rhythm of your breathing. Inhale deeply and exhale through your nose. For the next few minutes, place all of your awareness on your breathing. Then, when the time feels right, and as you continue to breathe slowly, begin to imagine a funnel-shaped golden light descending from the heavens above your head. This golden light flows into your body. Visualize it melding into every part of your body—from your head, down your neck, your arms, hands, chest, back, torso, legs, and feet. Imagine that every cell and muscle, and your entire bloodstream are being filled with this golden light. It fills your entire body and transmutes other people's energy, depressed feelings, and negative thinking into a positive, loving energy. Imagine all the limited, gloomy energy as specs of dirt coming out from your fingertips and toes, and falling down into Mother Earth.

Visualize releasing all bitterness and resentment, until you feel very clear. In a few minutes, you will begin to feel a lightness traveling through your body. Feel this golden energy running up and down your spine, brightening your entire being. After sitting with this feeling of lightness for a while, place your awareness at the center of your chest. Become conscious of the beating of your heart. Picture yourself in the center of your heart, so that you become part of your heartbeat.

Next, imagine a bright green light emerging from your heart and forming a life-size green crystal ball in front of you. This green light from your heart is made of unconditional love and healing. Now, place a person that you need to forgive in the spirit world inside this green crystal healing ball. Let the person know you love him or her unconditionally. As you begin to forgive, you will feel a difference in your body. You may begin to cry, or start to sneeze or cough. This is normal. You are letting go of old stagnant energy that you had associated with this person. Energy is shifting.

After a few minutes, begin to place another person in the center of the green crystal healing ball. Send this person the feeling of unconditional love and forgiveness. This can also be someone in the living world that you have not forgiven. Perhaps it is your wife or husband, the drunk driver, or any person you think was responsible for your child's death. After a few minutes, replace the image of the last person with yourself standing in the middle of the green crystal healing ball. As you look at yourself, you will begin to see your features take on a younger appearance. In this moment, let the healing inside you. Love yourself unconditionally, as you have the others. You are made of God's loving energy. Recognize it; enjoy it; and forgive yourself. When you are ready, open your eyes. Whenever you feel down, remember this green healing ball of energy. It will reenergize you.

The Gift Box Meditation

In my daylong and weekend workshops, I do many meditations that help people meet with loved ones, and they are very effective. The important thing to remember before embarking on any meditative journey is to stay out of your head/ego and let the energy flow in order to experience Spirit without expectations. You want to receive; you do not want to control. Just as in the previous meditation, make sure you are in a place without interruptions for at least a half hour. Close your eyes, and begin to align yourself with your body, becoming aware of how it feels without judging it.

Once again, bring your awareness to your breath, paying particular attention to each inhalation and exhalation. With each inhalation, imagine the golden light of heaven coming into the top of your head and moving through your entire body. Feel the light in each muscle, cell, and tissue. As you breathe in and out, your mind begins to slow down, and you enter a place of neutrality. When you feel centered in your being, use your imagination to go on a celestial journey.

See yourself in a colorful hot-air balloon. With each inhalation, the balloon rises higher. With each exhalation, it rises higher and higher. After several breaths, you find yourself drifting above the clouds in a world that you have never seen before. It is a world of pristine beauty and dazzling color. Each color tells a story. Just for a few moments, immerse yourself in this environment, taking in its magic and feeling how the different colors affect your being. Off in the distance, beyond the clouds, you see a garden filled with a variety of flowers that seem to glimmer like an array of diamonds.

Your hot-air balloon very gently touches the vibrant green grass of the garden, and immediately you have a sense that this is *your place*. You step out of the balloon and, with all of your senses, you begin to take into your awareness this new garden world. This is your spiritual garden. It represents your spiritual self. Feel how alive and vivid everything is. This place represents your inner beauty, your inner guidance, and your higher self. You feel love all around you. Your guide or guides come to greet you, and you are happy to see them. Notice how they are dressed. You may not have known your guides before, and you are very happy to meet them for the first time. You communicate through thoughts and realize that you are in a world of peace, oneness, and endless possibilities. It is a blank canvas on which you can create whatever you like.

As you become more in tune with your celestial world, you look off in the distance and see figures of people. Your guides are leading them toward you. The first thing you notice are their eyes, then the rest of them comes into focus. These are your loved ones—your children, mothers, fathers, partners, relatives, friends, and even animal family that have passed into the light. As you move toward them, you notice how young and vibrant they are. Feel their energy and their love. Suddenly, comfortable benches appear on which to rest. You and your loved ones sit, and you spend precious moments together. As with your guides, you communicate with them through thought. You have done this many times before, and it feels so natural to you. You notice that your loved ones have created a special hand-carved box just for you. It is covered with precious jewels—sapphires, diamonds, rubies, and emeralds. The box has your name on it; it represents you and seems to be an extension of you.

At this time, ask your loved ones a question. It should be something that you have stored deep in your heart—a question for which you have not received an answer. When you know you are ready for the response, slowly open the box and look inside. The answer may come in the form of words, phrases, colors, symbols, or pictures. Sit with the gift a while. If you choose to continue communication, do so.

When you are ready to return to the awareness of your physical body, take a deep breath and become instantly aware of your feet on the ground and your connection to Mother Earth. Next, be aware of how different your physical body feels. Then become aware of your heart and your emotional self. You may want to write your insights in a notebook and review these words and images from time to time, knowing that your spirit family is just a breath away.

You Did Your Best, Mom

Recently, I did the gift box meditation at an Omega Workshop, and I received the following letter from one of the people in attendance.

Dear James,

. . . You guided us into a beautiful garden where we were introduced to our guides. At that point, we requested their assistance to meet our loved ones. My son appeared as clearly as if he were alive again—happy, free of pain, and whole—just like he was before his illness ravaged his body. He was with my mom and dad, with Chip standing in the front. I knew that my parents understood the importance of me seeing my son alive again. I knew that they understood the extreme need a parent has when she loses a child. They were standing behind Chip to assure me that they were with him and they were all together.

You then told us that one of our loved ones held a jeweled box, and that there was a gift within this jeweled box for us when we were ready to receive it. Chip was holding the jeweled box. I asked him to bring it forward. He walked toward me and placed this most beautiful, glistening jeweled box in my lap. This beautiful ethereal gift was for me! The presentation of the gift was an impressive regal ceremony, as Chip got down on one knee, did an amazing royal bow, flaring his right arm out to the side, bowing his head with much pomp and circumstance, saying *For you, Your Majesty.*

I kept hearing and feeling over and over: *I love you Mom. You were the best, Mom. You did your best, Mom.* You then prompted us to open the box when we were ready. I opened the box and out flowed the following words in lovely ribbons, floating higher and higher. They were so light, they flew out of sight like balloons dancing in the air. *Abundance. Love. Happiness. Compassion. Grace. Health.* My heart was overflowing with gratitude and a depth of love that is beyond description.

Chip then placed his head on my knee, and I felt that feeling a mother feels when her child shows the genuine love he feels for her. Like a babe when, for the first time, he extends his little hand to your face. The love that I felt during this process cannot easily be explained, for it was fully outside of any life experience that I have had to date. I was in another place, another space. My heart was filled, the tears freely flowing down my face as Chip sat to my left side, placing his arm around my shoulders and resting his head next to mine.

My mother then stepped forward and sat on my right side, resting her head on my other shoulder. My dad joined us by embracing us all. Group hug! A visit with my son; a visit with my parents. Silence filled with harmonious beauty. Had I not attended this amazing forum where open minds consciously and powerfully brought together a concentrated force, I might never have felt this. I am forever grateful to you, James, for this

empowerment. It will never leave me. My life is changed.
I can live in peace. My boy is well, and he continues to
love me.

Anita

Support One Another

As Anita so wonderfully put it, getting together with other
people going through a similar experience helps to boost
our energy. There are many beneficial outlets for help and
guidance. Grief support groups are one. I urge everyone
who has gone through a loss to attend one. If you feel too
inhibited to attend a group, there are grief counselors who
will work one-on-one with you. Most churches, hospices,
and charitable organizations usually have information on
support groups and counselors. Of course, attending a spiritual seminar, retreat, or weekly spirit circle can be very
supportive.

A woman who attended my spirit circle in Laguna Beach
wrote that, each time she attended the circle, she came away
feeling so much better about her son in the spirit world. "I
really feel you helped me to realize that death isn't the end,
just life in a different form." Another woman wrote that the
loss of her child led her to volunteer at the Court Appointed
Special Advocate program, working with children in the foster
system. As she said, she would probably never have done this if
her son hadn't passed and begun pushing her in Spirit to move
in new directions. "When I fall into the abyss of grief, my son
comes to comfort me, and I realize that this is but a time apart.
I seek a way to let other parents on this path know that we can
survive the loss of our children. It isn't easy, but there is a way
to move forward and to accept what is. We can see a lovely

sunset and still appreciate that God's hand is in everything and that we're meant to find our way."

In one way, supporting others can help us to start feeling better. I received an e-mail from one mother who found her own kind of support group at one of my demonstrations.

Dear James,

My journey began with the passing of my twenty-one-year-old daughter, Liz. My religious beliefs no longer offered the comfort that they had in the past. In my quest to make sense of events that occurred, I began reading books that offered me a chance to look at life through a new lens. I read many books by you.

I had the good fortune to attend a soul retreat weekend with you in New York City. To attend such a workshop was something new for me. A year later, a good friend attended a seminar with you and we made plans to attend your seminar together when you returned. The weekend of your seminar was everything I thought it would be. As it was winding down, you promised a few closing readings.

You began to read for a woman sitting directly behind me. Her name was Betty, but you called her Beth (my name) several times. Her daughter Vicky, who had passed less than a year after my daughter, was coming through. You gave her many specific details. You said that she enjoys watching the family release balloons in her honor, and is happy that the family is setting up a foundation in her name. She (her spirit) ended by telling her mom to say hi to Flo, her mom's best friend.

The reason I am noting Betty's reading is that all of the above also applied to me—right down to: Say hi to

Flo, my good friend sitting next to me who led me to you
in the first place. When Flo asked you to explain how
the reading also applied to me, and that my name was
Beth, you said that our daughters had orchestrated their
mothers' attending the workshop. You said that they had
become good friends, and were laughing and having a
good time together. It was their plan to have their moms
meet.

   This event occurred one and a half years ago. Betty
and I have stayed in touch and will continue to. I know
she will be in my life forever. I really can't believe how
much we think alike. Not only do I enjoy her company
immensely, but I feel that she is one of the few people
who understands completely what my life is like—and
vice versa. She can make me laugh, and I consider her a
good friend. We have no doubt that our girls are friends,
because, as we share stories, it is apparent that they were
and are so much alike.

   As a result of my weekend with you, I am much more
able to make sense of the passing of my courageous,
beloved daughter, and have come to see the lessons that
her life and death have taught me. I know my daughter is
watching over our family and that she wants us to heal
and live happy and productive lives in her honor.

   Beth M.

P.S. You asked to speak with Betty and me privately
after our reading. You continued to reassure us that our
daughters were nearby. Then you had someone take a
picture of us, which I have attached. Notice the many
orbs that surround the three of us.

Helping one another go through the same thing, as these two women have done, can be like a mini support group. There are many websites with grief support information, including my own. Take the first step by getting help and support as soon as you can.

Spiritual Change

A child's death can cause a major spiritual change in a parent. Many of the letters I receive are about spiritual awakenings. Often, people change their religious beliefs or find new spiritual understanding outside mainstream religious organizations. Some grow more religious and get more involved in their church. Some go to psychics and healers for guidance and support. Some attend New Age spiritual groups. Many find spiritual empowerment in the depths of their grief. Some find God and a direct connection to Spirit. Here is how one mother changed.

> Dear James,
>
> I can tell you from my heart what a wonderful feeling it is to be able to connect with my deceased child in Spirit. I have been reading about spirituality since my son passed, but I have to say that your reading changed my life like no other book or spiritual event I've encountered. I took your online course "Enhancing Your Intuition," and it has opened my spirituality door and my connection to Spirit.
>
> Messages of love and support mingled with my acceptance to connect. Belief and intention in connecting to Spirit has gifted me with visions, sounds, and messages

from Spirit. I feel that my life prior to this connection
was a mundane rerun. Now I feel as if my life's door has
opened to a brand-new world of wonder and excitement.
I once was a church member, as a child with my parents,
but have never felt that I needed the support of a church
to sustain my being. I have always believed in God and
Jesus, but when I had a vision of Jesus two nights in a
row, I knew for sure that my future was to serve Spirit.
I can say that I am on a mission to share with the world
God's connection to us all, and the unconditional love
Spirit has for each and every one of us.

    Janet

Affirmations

I always like to close my readings, workshops, events, and television shows with affirmations, because I want everyone to
leave the experience on a high spiritual vibration. So I will
close this chapter in the same way. Affirmations are positive
statements spoken aloud in the present tense to achieve a de-
sired state. Remember that your thoughts are real things! Like
attracts like; therefore, what you send out in thought and word,
you will receive back. Thoughts carry an amazing amount of
creative energy and manifest into reality if you dwell on them
long enough. Before I get out of bed each day, I program my
mind with positive and loving energy.

    I have put together a list of affirmations for you to use if you
like. You can pick a favorite one or make your own. Use these
affirmations as stepping stones to get you started thinking in
a positive way. I do affirmations in the morning when I brush
my teeth, and the same at night. It is interesting to note that if

you want to write, begin a sentence with an affirmation. You will open up, and probably write a lot more. Just go with it and see what happens. The most important thing to remember is that the more you use affirmations, the stronger and quicker the results will materialize in your life.

START OF A NEW DAY

Each day brings with it new hope and lessons to learn.
Everything shall come to pass in God's time. I am just
    helping it along.
I am in charge of my life.
My loved ones are and always will be a part of my daily
    life.
I go inside myself and discover my soul.
Being alone forces me to discover how great I am.
As I acknowledge my loss, I confirm my love for ____.
Life is a constant dance. I move now, because tomorrow I
    may not remember the steps!

GRIEVING

I am open to receiving healing in every aspect of my life.
I have gratitude for the soul lessons I have been taught by
    this experience.
I am beginning to heal just by acknowledging my grief.
I am open to feel and live this loss fully.
I acknowledge that life is now different, not good nor bad,
    just changing.
Loss is a part of the life experience.
I can grieve as I choose.
I am never alone.
A broken heart opens up to more love.
I am divinely guided in all that I do in my life.

I take the next step with confidence and love myself fully.
I look forward to the wonderful new experiences that
tomorrow brings.

It is very interesting that, after you start using affirmations,
you can't help but have an attitude adjustment that impacts
every aspect of life. You may think you are saying affirmations
for grief, yet you soon find that other aspects of your life feel
more alive and freeing. Eventually, you will come back to the
ultimate truth, no matter what life throws at you. You are and
always will be *love*.

No one travels the journey alone. If you, like many of the
parents who have written to me, can recognize that your
child has given you a spiritual opportunity, you will survive
and thrive on your journey. You will be transformed in your
human experience on these earthly shores. There may be times
of deep sorrow and pain, but your child is always close by to
strengthen you with courage. The bonds of love last through
eternity.

9

Letters from
Heaven

*We are given children to test us and
make us more spiritual.*

— GEORGE F. WILL

I T IS IMPORTANT that you realize that your child is alive
and well in another dimension. Even if you cannot understand where or what this means, it does not alter the fact
that they can hear your thoughts quite clearly and concisely.
Over the years, Spirit has given me various exercises to help
others realize that their loved ones are close by. One of my
favorites is a letter-writing exercise between parents and their
children. I have found that letter writing is one of the best ways
to carry on a continued communication with a loved one, no
matter what your belief system is. Having preconceived ideas
of a Christian-based heaven, however, may limit your experience and that of your loved one. As you will read, many children in the higher side of life do not find a Christian heaven,
even though they may have been taught to believe in one at a

young age. In order for this exercise to be successful, you must be open to the love that passes between you and your child. This is a wonderful opportunity to reconnect with your loving child, who is merely beyond the veil of your limited senses.

First, pick a day in your calendar when you can write your letter. On that date, find a place where phones, computers, TVs, or people wanting your attention will not disturb you. You will need paper, a pen, and an envelope. When you are comfortable, and before putting pen to paper, take a few moments to center yourself. Take a few deep breaths and let your mind and body relax. When you feel calm, think of what you want to say to your child. Imagine that your child resides in a foreign country, and you have only three minutes to speak on the phone. What would you say? What would you ask? Try to ask questions that have meaning for you. Some people tend to write basic questions like: Where are you? How do you feel? Who is with you? What are you doing there? Do you visit me? Let your words come from your heart, but try not to let your emotions get in the way, as they may block the reception of the one to whom you are writing. Don't overthink or overanalyze your letter; just let it flow. Make sure you begin the letter the way you would any letter. Write the date, and then Dear. . . . Write as long a letter as you can in three minutes, trying to be as clear and concise as possible.

Sometimes people like to enclose a memento with the letter. This can be a prayer card or photo, petals from a flower, or a piece of jewelry. Mementos are not at all necessary, but if you want to include one, then do it. When you are finished writing your letter, make sure to fold it up and place it in the envelope, then write your loved one's name on the front. Some parents have addressed their letters with "Heaven's Little Angel," or "The Seventh Cloud on the Right," or "God's Little

Messenger." All of that is okay, but the name will do just fine as well. Once you have enclosed the letter in the envelope and addressed it, put the letter away—perhaps in a drawer that you rarely open. It is important that you leave the letter untouched for at least one week. This means that you don't look at it.

The next step is to go back to your calendar and make an appointment to receive the return letter from your spirit child. Write down a date and time. Make sure you have it in your mind so you won't forget. You are making a very important appointment. Then release the letter from your mind, and let your wishes and desires go off into the ether.

When the date arrives for you to receive a letter back from your child, make sure you have plenty of paper and, once again, make very sure that you will not be disturbed. You may place a picture of your loved one in front of you if you wish. When you are ready to receive the reply—or, as I like to say, "transmission from Spirit"—take several deep breaths and relax into a state of neutrality. As you breathe and begin to center yourself, meditate on your loved one until you feel your body and mind relax deeply. In your mind, say his or her name three times. Place your pen on the paper and let your mind be filled with the thoughts of your spirit child. Let the message fill the page. Do not think about what you are writing; just let your mind freely flow onto the paper.

As you write the response letter, you will receive a sort of "spark" or "inspiration." That is Spirit connecting with you. You may be shocked by the messages that come through, be-cause they may not be what you expected. This is the most common comment I hear from my clients. Continue to go with the flow. When you are finished with the session, you will in-tuitively feel the energy shift and dissipate. Take a few breaths, then fetch the letter you sent. Open your letter first and read it;

then read the response letter. You will probably see how much it ties in with your original letter. Some people find this shocking, but it is very natural. As each of us is an energy field, this is a way to share our energy in a mind-to-mind communication.

Clients have asked me if this exercise is a form of automatic writing. Yes, it is. Essentially, this form of writing is done in an altered state of consciousness. Automatic writing was very popular at one time as a means of contacting the spirits and receiving their messages. It is believed that spirits use the writing utensil and can write through you. Years ago, I was told in a séance that my guides come through me when I write a book. As I lift my fingers on the keyboard, as it were, their words manifest on the page. I believe that everyone is a medium in varying degrees, and that many of the great works of music, literature, and theater came from automatic writing. The creators of these works are really channeling the ideas from Spirit, because all is created there first and on the physical plane last.

When doing the letter exercise, or using other forms of automatic writing, you may notice that your penmanship changes. That is the spirit of the person coming through your writing. The success of this exercise depends on a deep altered state of consciousness. That is why it is a good idea to meditate before receiving the response, so that you are using your right, receptive, brain and not your left, critical, brain.

Following are some letters between parents and their children in spirit. In publishing these intimate letters, my intention is to share with you the incredible insights from children who have passed into the higher side of life. They simply explain the truth of life in the spiritual dimensions. I hope they will also provide you with an enormous amount of comfort, healing, and insight, as they did to the parents who wrote and received them. I have chosen to change the names of the letter owners and did my best to keep them in the correct order. I think they will give you a wonderful sense of what life is like for children growing up in heaven.

Letters to Spirit—Answers from Heaven

February 14, 1999

To My Dearest Little Monkey,

It has been five years since you left us from this world and moved into your heavenly home with Jesus. I know you were an angel on this earth for a short time. I am blessed and so happy to have shared our seven years together, but I understand God called you home. I pray for you every day and seem to miss you more and more. I wonder if I will ever have a normal life again. Your sister, Ella, loves you very much and kisses your picture before going to sleep at night. Do you watch over us? Have you seen Grandma Sally and Grandpa Joe? I wish so much to hold you! Nobody here understands the pain I still feel every day without my precious monkey in my life, and the joy we shared together. No one ever loved me like my little monkey. I just came across your fifth-birthday-party pictures and cried so much. You had your usual big smile and deep-brown eyes. Boy, the camera loved you! I hope you could see me visiting the cemetery with the balloons for your birthday. Somehow I feel closer to you there. Not a day goes by that I do not think of you. I look forward to the day Jesus calls me home to be with you again, and we can continue playing in heaven.

I love you now and always!

Mommy

February 21, 1999

Dear Mommy,

I love you more and more every day. Time goes by fast, at least on earth, but not where I am. It just is. I guess I would be twelve in earth time. I love it when you write me letters, even though I am standing over your shoulder watching you do it. Mom, I remember what you told me about heaven and Jesus, but I have not found him yet. People tell me he is in a higher place. I thought heaven was going to be filled with angels and harps, but I have not seen them yet. Mr. McArthur takes care of me. I guess you could say he is my spiritual parent. Grandpa and Grandma picked him out for me. He is such a nice man. I play sports here all the time—baseball, soccer, and games I never knew on earth. You would be proud of me. I am in a school studying science. It is a different type of science than on earth, so I'm told, but I love knowing why things happen. Mom, I am sorry you feel so sad. Please be happy. I am. I loved the balloons, but I am not in the ground. You know that, right? I am like the balloons floating in the air. I am with you every day. I come with a lot of people, and we try and cheer you up. I do my monkey dance in front of you hoping you will see it. I can't wait for you to come here, Mommy, and see the colors. There are so many more than you could ever imagine. Tell Ella that I watch her and kiss her goodnight every night when she rests her head on the pillow. Mommy, watch for me in your dreams. I will bring you a big monkey.

Love, Ben

October 9, 2008

Dear Jenna,

I feel as if I am still in some sort of a nightmare with you no longer living here by our side. I feel guilty for buying you the car that ended your life. I should have known better. Isn't that what a mother is supposed to know? I am sorry you will not be going to college, as you looked so forward to getting your degree in music and perhaps one day composing. I still remember how you insisted that we buy you a piano when you were only four. Little did we know we had a musical genius in our midst. I am truly very sorry that you did not live to see your dream come true. I hope you are with Aunt Mary and Papa; they loved you so much. Please help your daddy out. He has been very depressed, and he seems to be getting worse. I love you so much and hold your sweater every day.

Love, Mom

October 16, 2008

Dear Mom,

I miss you every day, too. I miss your trying to get me out of bed for school and telling me I'll be grounded if I don't get up. I also miss your telling me not to use my cell phone at the table. Boy, I was bad, huh? I miss

Dad, too. Please tell him that I know he is sad. When I
stand beside him, I can feel his tears from the inside. If
he only knew where I was, his heart would be as full as
mine. I know that you feel bad about buying me that car,
but I love you for that. You are such a caring and loving
mom, and you knew I would love the car. So please don't
be mad at yourself. You did nothing wrong. Believe it
or not, I was supposed to die the way I did. The drunk
driver who hit me did it to teach us all about forgiveness.
Please forgive him. His mind is full of darkness, and he
needs your prayers. Mom, you would love it here. Music
is everywhere. I am studying music in a sort of finishing
school. I guess you could call it that. All the students
learn how to express themselves individually in music,
and then we blend our tones together. You can walk in a
valley and hear beautiful music everywhere. It is heavenly.
I am learning to play the oboe. Isn't that funny? I always
secretly wanted to. I have seen all of our family here, but
the most incredible one is Miss Whiskers! She was on my
bed when I woke up. I am very happy. I love you always!

   Love, Jenna

June 15, 2006
Dear Son,

   My heart aches so much—I don't know if I want to
live anymore. I was told by someone to sit down and
write you a letter and let my feelings out, and maybe, just
maybe, you would hear me. I don't know. It seems crazy.
Nothing else seems to work, so what the heck. Son, I feel
so bad about what happened. I should have been there
for you. I was only concerned about myself and not about

you or your sister. Please forgive me, because I cannot forgive myself. I should have been more present in your life. If I had been, I would have recognized that you had a drug problem. Well, that's not true. I had some idea, but I guess I just didn't want to admit it to myself. I wish I had been a better dad. If I had been, maybe you wouldn't have gotten in with a bad crowd. Life has so much to offer—not only the bad, but also plenty of good. I just wish you had had the chance to live some of it. I am so sorry to have let you down. I went through my drawer the other day, and you won't believe what I found—the picture of you and your old man at the father-and-son Boy Scout dinner. God, I was so proud. I'll always be proud of you, son. I wish we could go fishing again. Your mom misses you, too. I know she does, even though we don't talk much. Maybe if we hadn't divorced, things would have been more stable. I don't know. I will always have my memories. I hope there is a heaven. I pray that you are happy. You deserve the best. I am so sorry for not being able to save you. I wake up in the middle of the night crying. Please forgive me.

Your Loving Father, forever.

June 22, 2006

Dear Father,

I love you very, very much. I have always looked up to you as someone I wanted to be. You don't need to be forgiven. Please forgive me for leaving before I was supposed to. I messed up big time. I thought I was a big shot, but I know now that I was fooling myself. I blame myself, not you. I thought things would be better for me if I ended it, only to find that nothing ends the way we think. I have to work out my problems here just as I did on earth.

When I first got here, a whole group of people met me. Their job was to help new arrivals understand their new life. The ones that met me specialized in suicides. So many of us thought there would only be darkness. I was angry with myself and sad that I had blown my life. They really helped me get through it. Big time! There are lots of people like me with emotional problems. We all go to meetings and talk about our problems and how to deal with them. You will be relieved to know that my problem did not start with you, but many lifetimes ago. I carried the memory with me and had a chance to overcome my addiction, but fell into a dark place in my mind. I'm working on this problem so I don't have to repeat it.

I live in a dormitory with others who took their lives, and we all get along. No fights or disagreements. We all seem to be on the same page. Besides, we know what everyone is thinking and feeling. There are no secrets here. I am going to a university and studying a lot. It's really amazing. All I have to do is think about something, and it suddenly appears. I wish it were that easy back on earth. School and studying are very important. It seems everyone in my group is in school. It's different from school on earth. We study about love, how to watch out for each other, and how to help when someone gets in trouble. It's all about making these qualities part of your soul. It's very interesting. The classrooms are not anything like what I have seen on earth. The buildings are very classic and clean. We can also take class outside in one of the many beautiful gardens. There are no

ownership problems. Everything belongs to everyone.
Wouldn't that be great on earth? No one would have to
be afraid or worried anymore. One day I want to go back
to earth and help poor people.

Please tell Mom I love her. I am going to lead her to
the new Tiffany lamp she is looking for. Mom loves you
Dad. I think my death was so hard for her that she took it
out on you. Don't stop loving her. I have found that love
is the only way. Hey, I have created a picture of you and
myself fishing on the lake, and I look at it all the time. I
love you, Dad. I am always here for you.

Love you, Stu

December 25, 2001

My Little Precious Mellie,

Today is Christmas, and I can't stop thinking about
you. I have been so sad. I can still see your little body
and how sick you were. I hope the words I spoke in your
ear at the hospital were heard. I miss you very much.
Mommy and Daddy miss you, too. I am sorry for not
writing sooner. Sometimes it is hard for me. Please
forgive me. Thank you for coming to me in my dreams.
I love the beautiful garden, and the gardenias are my
favorites. Do you like little teddy I put inside your coffin?
I wanted to make sure you had your favorite toy with
you. It is cold outside and the snow is falling. It is a
beautiful white Christmas. I remember when you wanted
ice skates for Christmas, and Santa brought them to you.
You were so happy. I am sorry you were never able to use
them. Tomorrow you would have been eight. I hope you
are celebrating with all the angels in heaven. Say hello

from me to my brother, your great-uncle Billy. I love you.
I promise to write again.

XO,

Grandma

January 1, 2002

Dear Grandma,

I love you very much. Your letters come to me as
beautiful colors. I can see all your thoughts, even the ones
you forget to write down. I asked our caretakers here
what the colors mean. I was told that earth people send
us a lot of heart colors, so I guess that is what you send.
You send me pretty pictures every day when you think
of me, and I feel tingly all over. It is like dancing under
a waterfall, but not getting wet. I love it here, Grandma.
There are so many children from all different countries.
I remember learning about them in my geography class,
and how they all spoke different languages. Not here. We
all understand each other no matter where we came from.
My best friend is Mai. She came from China. We knew
each other right away, because we had been best friends
before.

I loved making that dream for you. I am glad you liked
the flowers. It's easy for me to come to you in dreams,
because we are together in my world, not your earth
world. I have lots of toys to play with. The toy makers
here make them from love. I can feel the love every time I
play with them. I did see little teddy you put next to me,
and I have a teddy bear here on my dresser. Some of the
children create Santa Claus in this world, the same as on
earth. Everything is done so easily by just thinking of it.

I have not been ice-skating because there is too much to do. I just came from visiting lands with great animals—the ones with big bodies and big teeth. There were lions, wolves, and lots of bears. I love bears—especially the white ones. I can pet them here. You can't do that on earth. They know no one can hurt them here, so they roam freely and are not afraid the way they are in your world. Grandma, when you come here, you will see how natural it all is. Please give kisses to Mom and Dad. I will be with you in your dreams.

I love you always.

Hugs, Mel

March 10, 2009

Dear Sweet Baby Kari,

I love you a lot. Even though we never met on earth, you are always in my thoughts. I wanted you so much, but it could not be. I was too sick, and you were too tiny to live. I feel so guilty that I wasn't strong enough to help you be born. I live with the guilt and sometimes I get so depressed. I wonder where you are and if you are somewhere in heaven. I wonder if you ever think of me. Your sisters and brother also ask me where you went. I tell them that God had bigger plans for you. You were needed to turn the stars on at night and work closely with the heavenly angels. I only wish that it were so. There must be a reason why you had to leave. I will never forget you. I carry you in my heart. Let me know if you are with me and watching over us.

Love,

Your Mommy

March 17, 2009

Dear Mommy,

I love you all a lot, too. I am around you whenever you think of me. I live with all the babies, and the angels take care of us. The angels always take care of the babies who return to heaven. When you see me on this side, I will be all grown up. I have learned to walk already. I don't have to talk, because we only have to think, and everyone can do that no matter how young they are. Don't feel sad. It hurts to feel you in pain. It wasn't your fault. I knew I wouldn't be born. I only wanted to feel what it was like to be back in a body, and I didn't like it. I have to learn not to be so afraid. My angel said I could help you a lot more from this world. When you look up at the stars at night and say goodnight to me, I am looking back at you. I can feel the love you have for me. I will stay close by, because I promised you I would.

I love you very much.

Kari

July 4, 2005

Dear Bryan,

I am sitting here in the living room, staring at the flag they gave me at your service. I can hardly fathom that you will not be coming through the back door and reaching out to hug me. I miss you and feel so lost without you. My heart has been torn out of my chest. People are still calling me with condolences, and sending beautiful cards and pictures of you. I feel that I could open a museum. I have many of the photos on the table next to a candle. I hope you can see them. Dad spends most of his time in the garage. I have to bring his dinner out there. He is so heartbroken that he cannot speak, not even to me. I don't know how to help him, because I am in so much pain myself. Your sister has been coming over a lot and helping out.

I know you didn't believe much in religion, or that we go on after death, but I hope you are in a beautiful place. I pray this is true. Your life was short; you were just twenty when you left us. The day you were born is vividly etched in my mind. We were rushing to the hospital because you were coming so fast. You could have been born in the backseat if we hadn't gotten to the hospital when we did. I guess you could not wait to come into this world. You were always strong-willed, determined, and ready to tackle anything. I guess that is why you joined the Marines. You taught your father and me so much in your short time here, and I hope we have done the same for you. Did you see us at the cemetery yesterday? They keep the place so pristine. Please let me know what you are doing and give me a clue when you are around. I want to know that you are all right. I don't believe you are dead, but very much alive.

Love forever,
Mom

July 11, 2005
Dear Mom,

I am always with you, so don't feel that you are ever alone. I hug you when you wake up and sit beside you when you have your eggs in the morning. Sometimes, you

look right at me as though you feel me next to you. It is
me! Do you remember when you thought you smelled
my after-shave lotion? That was me. I tried to send you
something that you would associate with me. I will try to
make the connection stronger next time. That's my sign
that I am by your side.

I don't remember how I died; it happened so suddenly.
It took me a while to understand what had happened.
My body was blown to bits, but I was still there. My
spirit was still there. I could see soldiers in my unit
scattered all around. That's when I knew I was dead,
but I didn't feel as if things had ended. Actually, I felt
as if I were just beginning something new. The next
thing I saw was a group of Marines coming toward me.
I was confused, because I didn't know who any of these
guys were. They told me I had a new assignment called
Spirited. A colonel informed me that I had finished my
assignment in the body, and that it was time to report to
the spirit side of life. He told me I had work to do and
that I was to help the other soldiers in my troop cross
over. So I began to walk around the area to meet the
soldiers who had died. Like me, they were traumatized.
I realized that I was not alone; there were others helping
me in my assignment and they were not soldiers, but
the civilians we had just killed. At first, it was strange,
but they were not different from me. In fact, they were
actually a part of me. We all felt sad that life had to
end this way. Together, we worked for quite some time
assisting new arrivals to recognize their fate. Some were
able to handle it, but a few needed further help. You
would be proud of me. Yes, I now believe in the afterlife.
I am proof.

Since I've been here, I have been very busy. Fortunately, I have been able to do whatever my heart desires. I am very interested in history, and I have been able to meet various souls from past times to discuss the reasons for war and the need to overpower one another. I have been touring the lower spirit realms on a regular basis. It's like being on skid row, because there are so many souls that still feel hate toward others and want to kill them. These poor souls are truly lost. They don't believe in themselves. You might even say they are damned. I am drawn there to counsel these souls and to help them realize they can get better. I am also in charge of a group of souls who have died from drugs. It's amazing—they still think they are high—that is, until I break the news to them. Many spirits support my efforts, including Uncle Bob. We visit governments on earth to persuade people in charge to use peaceful ways to achieve what they wish. I now know that war and killing are not highly evolved ways of thinking. It took me some time to forgive myself for killing others, because I saw how we are all connected.

Thanks for all the photos. I will try to show myself in one of them the next time. Look for the lights.

I love you,
Bryan

P.S. Tell Mike I love his new motorcycle.

May 16, 2000
My Darling April,

Every sunrise and sunset, I call your name and talk to you, knowing how much you loved to see the colors.

You were just fourteen years old when you left the safety and love of your home here in California. Chris and Jeff miss you terribly, but they don't like to talk about you. Maybe they don't want to believe it is true. I know they are hurting inside. They lost not only their sister, but their best friend as well. Chris still wears your hat all the time, and Jeff still puts on your board shorts. We have dedicated a skateboard park in your name, and the boys have made a shrine around your surfboard. We look at the videos all the time and I still listen to your voicemail on my phone. I will never erase it. We all miss seeing you in our dreams. The boys have not seen you in almost a year; for me, it's been even longer. Why is that? We used to dream of you more often after you died. Your dad said to me the other day that he wants to return to Hawaii, and that you would probably want us to, but I still have bad feelings about it. What do you think? I wanted to ask you if you came to me the other day with my mother. I smelled her rose perfume and also thought of you. I hope Grandma is taking good care of you. We miss you very much. You are always in our thoughts.

Love forever,
Mom

May 23, 2000

Aloha Mama!

You caught me again! You know me, always running around traveling. You never let me get away with anything—even now when I am in spirit form. Ha, ha. I love you, Daddy, and my brothers so much. I wish I could share all the awesome discoveries that I have been experiencing here. Some would blow your mind. Others would be too hard to describe to you. Let's just say that nature here is made of the highest of colors. It reminds me of the rainbow waterfalls in Hawaii. Everything happens in such perfect harmony with everything else. There is this great Universal balance.

You know how much I love the water. Well, I have this great home right on the beach. It's so magical here, because it is always daylight and the weather is totally perfect. I am happy that my life ended while I was surfing. How perfect was that! There was no other place I would rather leave my body than in the water. Thanks for the rad going-away service. It was awesome! I especially loved it when everyone threw carnations into the surf. Yes, Mom, I was visiting you with Grandma the other day. She comes down from her place in the mountains to see me. She is in another part of this world. That day, she insisted on bringing you roses. She taught me that whenever I want to impress an earthly mind, I need to be very detailed in my thoughts. That's the way you can recognize us. She brought you a huge bunch of red roses—not your earthly red, but a really awesome red. We sent thoughts of these special roses from our minds to yours, and you got it. Cool!

Hey, I am sorry I have not been in your dreams lately. I have been real busy. Besides studying different forms of life in various stages of existence from the ocean to a whole star system, I have been making preparations to return to earth. It won't be for a while, as I love everything about this place. I have been listening to lectures, going to classes, and talking with my instructors about things I have to learn. I have been taking a look at different lives and trying to decide which one would be the most meaningful. I am leaning toward living in a jungle in my next earth life, but I'm not sure yet. My soul needs some experiences in remote places. Well, I am off. Tell Chris and Jeff thanks for the shrine. I am going to catch a wave.

Love you all, April

March 9, 2010

Dear Angie (short for angel)

It has been two years, and I don't know if you are alive or dead. It is impossible for me to sleep since you went missing. Even when I fall asleep, I wake up two hours later wondering where you are, and if you are still alive. I don't even know why I am writing this letter, but I cannot sleep. I am worried about you. Maybe if I get all the disturbing thoughts off my mind, I will feel better in some way, but I doubt it. I remember that day in November as if it were yesterday. It was like every other morning, except that I had a feeling in the pit of my stomach that something wasn't right. I wish I had listened to that hunch—not that I would have known what to do or what it was about anyway. I just knew something did not feel right. I remember making sure you took your sweater to school, because it looked as if it might snow. When you didn't come home that night, I knew that I would never see you again. Oh, baby, I am so sorry I could not have prevented this horrific situation. I pray every night that I will see you again, but I know deep in my heart I won't. There has been news from the detectives—they think you were kidnapped and taken to Canada. They think you are dead. But I don't want to accept it, even though they showed me the sweater I gave you. I am so sorry. If you are in heaven, I pray that the Lord has taken you under his arm and led you to a beautiful place where you will feel no pain. I will always have a candle lit in the window until I see you again.

Love Always and Forever,
Your Mother

March 16, 2010
Dear Mother,

Yes, your heart was right. I have left the cold, hard ground of earth and have found my glory in heaven. I am no longer walking in my body, for my body was lost a long time ago in a river north of our house. I don't even know if they will ever find it, but it doesn't matter. Mother, I am happy. I miss you and Dad very much and want you to know it was not your fault. I was foolish to trust someone I didn't know. I don't remember what happened. My last memory of earth was lying in a barn, and there was water behind me. I knew I would not stay alive very long, because I was weak. My head hurt so much from the hole in it. I went to sleep and woke up in a field of daisies. Auntie Ethel was sitting by my side. Everything was light, but the light wasn't coming from the sun. It was a different type of glow. After I learned that I had left my earthly home, I asked Auntie Ethel if you would know I had passed. That is when Grandpa Peter came to me and said that one day I would write you a letter and tell you where I am. Well, here it is.

I don't know how long I have been here, since time does not exist where I am, but I have been doing many things. I have several guides, or I guess you would call them teachers, and they say I am an evolved soul, and because of that, I need to help others. So, my guides have taken me to several places, from thatched-roof villages to palatial estates. I have met beautiful, happy, and charming people and some not very nice people.

One of the first places I went with my guide was to a dimly lit place. It was filled with spirits who had committed crimes on earth. My guide and I spent time with these criminal types and let them tell their stories. The man who kidnapped and killed me was there. My guide asked me to forgive him for what he had done to me. At first I could not. I could not feel any love in his energy field. When I listened to his thoughts, I understood why he did what he did. He was mentally ill. That's when I felt very sorry for this man with a sick mind.

All of the people in this dark land have problems—some given to them by their parents, and others by society. Each one needs help, and that's where I come in. I find out why they don't love themselves and encourage them to see themselves in a different light, so to speak. My guide tells me that I am doing such a good job in understanding their needs. Now, there are more volunteers who come with me, and I am their supervisor in a way. It is very rewarding to help these poor souls. The sad part is that many of them don't understand why they did what they did and had never been told they were loved on earth. I make sure they realize that there is a beautiful world beyond their dark home to experience.

This is all I can say now. I have to go. I want you to stop worrying about me, because I am alive, only not on earth. I am safe and happy. When you go to sleep tonight, you will finally be at peace. Tomorrow you will feel much better. I am with you more now than ever before.

I love you,
Ang (your little angel)

A Final Thought

Recently, I did a reading for a mother, Karen, and brought forth many messages from her daughter. After her daughter had passed, she received a poem from her, in much the same way some people receive letters. Her poem inspired me to write this chapter. Karen has kindly agreed to share her daughter's poem with all of us.

LETTER FROM HEAVEN

When I passed from here to there, I knew your heart
    would break.
It's here not there where I reside; in mountains, fields,
    and lakes.
In the break of each new dawn and when the sun goes
    down,
In birds and trees and skies of blue, you'll know I'm still
    around.
A broken heart I gave to you, no way to take that back;
Grieve for now, but don't stay long in the hole that's
    filled with black.
If I were there and you were here, you would clearly see

That you're right there and I'm right here, it's where we
    choose to be.
So dance and sing and laugh out loud, just like we
    always do;
I know it's hard, but you have to see that I'm right here
    with you.
And when you feel like crying, try and smile through
    the tears;
I hope you will remember, I'll love you for a thousand
    years.
And when you're feeling lonely, and you don't know
    what to do,
Just close your eyes and read this letter, from me to you.

Afterword:
A Step in Time

Recently, I was at an airport waiting for my plane to begin boarding. Instead of pounding my computer keyboard, or reading a book or magazine like the rest of the waiting masses, I sat back on an uncomfortable, faux-leather seat and stared at the milling, multitasking crowd walking back and forth in front of me. They ran to and from their gates, talked on cell phones, and lined up to buy food. Looking out at the sea of people, I wondered if there were others like me, sitting and observing others in their "natural" habitat and trying to imagine each one's life situation. As I scanned the crowd, a group of young boys ranging in age from seven to ten walked by, followed by their fathers. All of them were wearing baseball uniforms, so I assumed they were off to a baseball game. I caught the eye of one of the fathers and asked: "Championship game?" He proudly replied: "Yep. The series!" I wished him good luck, and he smiled and walked on.

As I watched the Little Leaguers move toward their gate, I was suddenly struck by a strong memory that brought me back to a time long ago. I was eight years old and sitting in my geography class, listening to my teacher chatter on about the various countries in South America. I was in the very back of the room, because my last name began with a V. Although it seemed unfair, even discriminatory, always to be stuck in the back because of my name, it certainly had its benefits as well. I was able to close my eyes without much notice from the teacher. On this particular occasion, I began to daydream about the Little League game I had played the night before, and I started to criticize myself.

The coach always sent me to the outfield because I was not very good at catching. I literally froze in my tracks thinking that everyone was looking at me and counting on me to make the catch, and I was mortified when I inevitably missed. On those rare occasions when I did catch the ball, I nervously dropped it out of my glove. As I was reliving this horror in my mind and thinking how I had let all those people down, I suddenly became aware of the spirit of a small blond-haired boy about my age coming through the middle floor-to-ceiling window of the classroom and walking over to me. He was dressed in a pin-striped uniform and a red cap, and he held a baseball glove.

The boy leaned toward me and whispered: *I'm Joey.* Then he went on to explain that he was a second baseman in the Springfield Little League.

He said: *I got dead in the fifth inning,* and I flashed on a ball hitting Joey right between the eyes. *My teachers told me to come here and talk to you. You're not seeing how good you are in the game.* He went on, saying that, instead of really enjoying the game, I was more concerned about what others thought of me. As this spirit stood beside me, I felt that time had stopped, and a telepathic link of communication opened between us.

I remember asking him, Who are you really? Why are you dressed like that?

He responded that he had gone back home to heaven over a year ago. *The last time I was on earth, I was the second baseman for Springfield.* He said that was the reason he chose to come back and show himself to me in his uniform. Joey talked about where he lived in the heavenly worlds.

You can visit me in your dreams, he insisted. *It is more real than this world.* I remember his saying that earth was like a "mirror" to our real home. He then pointed upward and said that there were so many things to do in heaven that no one on earth could ever imagine how special it was. *I wish my parents could see that I am alive.*

I didn't understand him. I kept thinking: But you're not alive, you're dead, and I'm the only one who can see you. Joey prattled on about how he was enjoying his life in heaven, and how his parents would be so happy for him; and if they knew, they would no longer spend all their time crying.

What exactly are you doing over there? I asked.

Growing and growing and growing! he answered.

I wanted to turn away from Joey, because he was giving me too many thoughts at once. My head was spinning as he shared all the information. I remember his telling me something about the soul experiencing everything from the past as well as the future.

Most people can't see who they really are on earth, but in heaven they can. At this point, I asked him to leave, but he insisted on telling me more.

I was just like you. I was afraid of letting people down. After I left earth, I realized the only reason I wanted to join Little League and play ball was to make my father love me more. It wasn't until after Joey died and was constantly bathed in the grief and tears of his father and mother that he realized his dad did love him. Joey just never knew it, because his father never told him.

My soul had to be born to my parents, because they would give me possibilities to learn about one of the windows of my soul, he said. I did not know what he meant, but I just felt that he was telling me that his parents were there to give him opportunities so he could learn about himself. And I felt from his communication that they had been together before.

I then very directly asked him: Are you an angel? In an instant, he "down-loaded" a sense of himself into my mind.

We are souls who live in many different places; like flowers, we grow everywhere. He tried to explain to me that some souls live and grow in heaven, which is made up of many places, and that earth is a place where we go to try and understand that we are souls.

We put on bodies and cover up our soul part, so we have to remember who we are. I tried to put two and two together about the reason for his visit. Was he trying to tell me not to worry about what others think or to remember that I am a soul?

Then Joey said it clearly: *You should never forget that you are a soul walking on the earth, so don't worry about what others think because they are souls too. You don't have to be afraid around other souls. You can shine your light for all to see.*

I am sure that I thought about it more simply then than I am remembering it now, but the feeling is the same. By *shine,* I think he meant "love," or to share love with others.

Do you still have to go to school in heaven? I asked him.

He laughed at me and said through his thoughts: *Yes, there are classes over here where we get to learn the pieces of our soul's puzzle.* He kept on trying to let me know that the boy I was seeing standing before me was only one aspect of who he was and that, in reality, he was made up of many different personalities who had lived all over this world and other worlds. I was completely thrown off by what he said to me. I did not understand any part of the conversation and kept on thinking: How could you have traveled around the world? You are a little boy!

At that moment, a loud bell interrupted my thoughts. It was time for a break, and I looked up as everyone ran out of class for recess. I was the last one in the room, and the teacher actually came over to help me. She looked down at me and asked: "Are you okay, James? Your face is as white as if you'd seen a ghost!" I think I said under my breath, "Maybe," and walked out of the classroom toward the playground.

Twenty minutes later, we returned to the classroom to resume our studies. I kept trying to see if Joey was around, but he was nowhere to be seen. I went through lunch, math class, and reading class, but Joey did not reappear. It was after two o'clock when the teacher told us to rest our heads on our desks for an afternoon break. As I closed my eyes and rested my head upon my arms, I heard a quick "pssst" sound. Out of the corner of my eye, I could see Joey. He was about an arm's length away from my face, staring right at me. He telepathically sent me the thought that he couldn't get through to me earlier because my mind was so busy and focused on class work that his thoughts got lost in the shuffle. He waited until I was receptive to him, so we would not be interrupted. He insisted that I keep my eyes closed in order to keep the link strong.

I want to show you something about what I said before. It's what our souls look like.

At eight years old, I really had no concept of what a soul was, but I was open to whatever he wanted to show me. In that moment, Joey impressed in my mind's eye a design and pattern that kept morphing and changing. At first, I saw a large square and inside the square were four more squares. Inside each quadrant of each square I could see a diamond connected to each side of the square. Then lines crossed through each diamond. The single quadrant became yet another quadrant, and the design continued to unfold, ad infinitum.

When he was ready to leave, Joey said: *This may not make sense to you now, but when you get older you will understand that this is the imprint of your soul, and each diamond is one lifetime that brings color to your being.*

Then, as quickly as he had appeared, he vanished. I was surprised, but mostly skeptical. I thought that I must have been dreaming the whole thing—that it was all in my head. School finally let out, and I was glad to get home. As soon as I walked in the door, I grabbed some paper and a pencil and began to draw my vision. Below is exactly what I had seen.

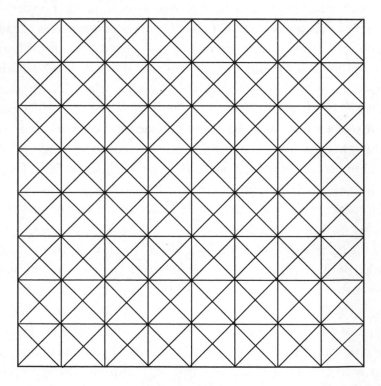

Soul Imprint

The most interesting thing about reliving this experience is what happened when I sat down to write the story. I had not seen the soul design since I was eight years old, so I was thrilled to remember this vision. A thought occurred to me that, if I put the outline of a human being in the middle of this design, the seven basic energy centers or chakras lined up perfectly in the exact middle of the diagram. It is quite amazing. Upon further contemplation, I realized each individual fragment represents an element (lifetime experience) within the soul's universal nature.

Little Joey is a reminder that we are all sacred, spiritual beings who never die. We are souls that grow and change, until we fully understand that we are perfect and beautiful beings.

Resources

Books

Addington, Jack and Cornelia Addington. *Your Needs Met.* Camarillo, CA: DeVorss, 1973.

Andrews, Ted. *The Healer's Manual.* Woodbury, MN: Llewellyn, 1993.

Barker, Elsa. *Letters from the Afterlife.* Hillsboro, OR: Beyond Words, 2004.

Bowman, Carol. *Return from Heaven.* New York: HarperCollins, 2001.

Dooley, Mike. *Infinite Possibilities.* New York: Atria Books/Beyond Words, 2009.

Finley, Guy. *The Secret of Letting Go.* Woodbury, MN: Llewellyn, 1998.

———. *Let Go and Live in the Now.* Berkeley, CA: Red Wheel/Weiser, 2004.

Fox, Emmet. *Power Through Constructive Thinking.* San Francisco: HarperOne, 1989.

Garfield, Laeh Maggie and Jack Grant. *Angels and Companions in Spirit.* Berkeley, CA: Celestial Arts, 1995.

Hay, Louise L. *The Power Is Within You.* Carlsbad, CA: Hay House, 1991.

Katafiasz, Karen. *Grief Therapy.* St. Meinrad, IN: Abbey Press, 1993.

Levine, Marie. *First You Die.* Silver Thread, 2004.

Noel, Brook and Pamela D. Blair. *I Wasn't Ready to Say Goodbye.* Kirksville, MO: Champion, 2000.

Moody, Raymond. *Life After Life.* New York: Bantam, 1976.

Morse, Melvin and Paul Perry. *Closer to the Light.* New York: Random House, 1990.

Newton, Michael. *Journey of Souls*. Woodbury, MN: Llewellyn, 1994.
———. *Destiny of Souls*. Woodbury, MN: Llewellyn, 2000.
———. *Memories of the Afterlife*. Woodbury, MN: Llewellyn, 2009.
Perkins, James Scudday. *Through Death to Rebirth*. Pasadena, CA:
   Theosophical Press. 1961.
Rhodes, Leon. *Tunnel to Eternity*. Woodbury, MN: Swedenborg
   Foundation, 1997.
Sanders, Catherine M. *How to Survive the Loss of a Child*. New York:
   Prima, 1992.
Schiff, Harriet Sarnoff. *The Bereaved Parent*. New York: Penguin, 1978.
Schwartz, Robert. *Your Soul's Plan*. Berkeley, CA: Frog Books, 2007.
Shaw, Eva. *What to Do When a Loved One Dies*. Irvine, CA: Dickens
   Press, 1994.
Shine, Betty. *Mind Magic*. New York: Bantam, 1991.
Shinn, Florence Scovel. *Your Word Is Your Wand*. Camarillo, CA:
   DeVorss, 1928.
Staume, David. *The Beginner's Guide for the Recently Deceased*.
   Woodbury, MN: Llewellyn, 2004.
Sutphen, Dick and Tara Sutphen. *Soul Agreements*. Newburyport, MA:
   Hampton Roads, 2005.
Tatelbaum, Judy. *The Courage to Grieve*. New York: HarperCollins,
   1984.
Tomlinson, Andy. *Healing the Eternal Soul*. Brooklyn, NY: O Books,
   2006.
Tweddell, Margaret Flavel and Ruth Mattson Taylor. *Witness from
   Beyond*. Chicago: Chicago Review Press, 1980.
Van Praagh, James. *Reaching to Heaven*. New York: Dutton, 1999.
———. *Healing Grief*. New York: Dutton, 2000.
Virtue, Doreen. *Healing with the Angels*. Carlsbad, CA: Hay House,
   1999.
Vogel, Gretchen. *Choices in the Afterlife*. Choices Publishing, 2010.
Wambach, Helen. *Life Before Life*. New York: Bantam, 1981.
White Eagle. *Sunrise*. Liss, UK: White Eagle Publishing Trust, 1958.
———. *Beautiful Road Home*. Liss, UK: White Eagle Publishing Trust,
   1992.
Zain, C. C. (Elbert Benjamine). *The Next Life*. Albuquerque, NM: The
   Church of Light, 1942.

Support Organizations

American Foundation for Suicide Prevention
120 Wall Street, 22nd Floor, New York, NY 10005
800-531-4477
Resources for suicide prevention and the survivors of suicide.
www.afsp.org

Baby Steps Children's Fund, Inc.
182-1054 Centre Street, Thornhill, ON, L4J 8E5, CANADA
905-707-1030
*Provides support and resources for families grieving the loss of
a child.*
www.babysteps.com

Bereaved Parents of the USA
PO Box 95, Park Forest, IL 60466-0095
708-748-7866
Self-help for bereaved parents, siblings, and grandparents.
www.bereavedparentsusa.org

The Compassionate Friends
PO Box 3696, Oak Brook, IL 60522-3696
877-969-0010
Provides support for families grieving the loss of a child.
www.compassionatefriends.org

Forever Family Foundation
222 Atlantic Avenue, Oceanside, New York 11572-2009
631-425-7707
*Provides support and healing for people in grief, and an
understanding of the afterlife.*
www.foreverfamilyfoundation.org

Good Grief Center for Bereavement Support
2717 Murray Avenue, Pittsburgh, PA 15217-2419
412-224-4700, 888-474-3388
Provides support for those in grief.
www.goodgriefcenter.com

Mothers Against Drunk Driving
511 E. John Carpenter Freeway, #700, Irving, TX 75062
800-GET-MADD
*An organization to stop drunk driving and to provide support for
family and friends of victims of drunk driving.*
www.madd.org

Parents of Murdered Children
   100 East Eighth Street, Suite 202, Cincinnati, Ohio 45202
   513-721-5683
   Provides support and assistance to all survivors of homicide victims.
   www.pomc.com
SHARE Pregnancy and Infant Loss Support
   402 Jackson Street, Charles, MO 63301
   800-821-6819
   A support organization for bereaved parents who lost their babies
   through stillbirth or miscarriage, and in the first few months of life.
   www.nationalshare.org
SIDS Alliance
   1314 Bedford Avenue, Suite 210, Baltimore, MD 21208
   800-221-SIDS
   Provides support for bereaved families suffering loss due to sudden
   infant death syndrome.
   www.sidsalliance.org

Internet Sites

www.crystalinks.com
   Information about karma, metaphysics, and reincarnation.
www.humanityhealing.net
   Information about the soul's purpose, soul families, and links to
   healing, grief support, and holistic healers.
www.near-death.com
   Provides resources and information for the purpose of understanding
   death.
www.nsac.org
   National Spiritualist Association of Churches.
   13 Cottage Row. PO Box 217, Lily Dale, NY 14752.
   Provides information about mediums and a national directory for
   spiritualist churches.
www.Vanpraagh.com
   Offers resources and links for bereavement and spiritual
   enlightenment, as well as community discussion chat rooms to
   support people in grief.

Acknowledgments

To all those beings both in Spirit and on the Earth, who have assisted me throughout the years in bringing my message of life after death out into the world. I thank and honor each one of you, especially:

Brian Preston, Boo Radley, Maizey Mae, Linda Tomchin, Ciaran and Kelly Barry, Joe Skeehan, Jacquie Ochoa-Rosellini, Heather Vogel, Kelly Dennis, Chip Mc Allister, Christian Dickens, Ken Robb, Tori Mitchell, Randy Wilson, Darlene Krantz, Bob Lewis, Cyndi Schacher, Gideon Weil, Suzanne Wickham, Scottie Schwimer, Jeff Eisenberg, Ron Oyer, Ciaran Sheehan, Gabrielle O'Connor, Marie Levine, Joerdie Fisher, Dorothea Delgado, Marilyn Whall, Liz Dawn, Cammy Farone, Angie Lile, Kim Keller, Rita Curtis, and Christy Lee

With deep appreciation to all the parents who have suffered the loss of their children and to those who have participated in my workshops, spirit circles and evening events. Thank you for sending me your heartfelt emails and postings to my web site.

Frank and Taunya Strocchio, Ann and Arnold Singer, Martha and Ernesto Chacon, Gail and Lance Harris, Lori Kizer, Glenda Walls, Norman and Babette Minery, Kathryn Musser, Deborah Matthews, Patricia Van Vliet, Jane Shaw, Joy M. and Joyce, Karen Cardenas James, and James Radford